ELIZAB1

THE CHRONICLES OF A MARKET TRADER'S DAUGHTER
FROM BLACKBURN

ELIZABETH

THE CHRONICLES OF A MARKET TRADER'S DAUGHTER FROM BLACKBURN

LIZ HODSON

ELIZABETH: The chronicles of a market trader's daughter from Blackburn

A Liz Hodson book
Revised edition published in Great Britain in 2019
Copyright © Elizabeth Hodson 2019
All rights reserved.

No part of this publication may be reproduced by any means, nor transmitted, nor translated into a machine language, without the written permission of the publisher.

The right of Elizabeth Hodson to be identified as the author of this work has been asserted in accordance with sections 77 and 78 of the Copyright, Designs and Patents Act 1988.

Condition of sale
This book is sold subject to the condition that it shall not by way of trade or otherwise be lent, re-sold, hired out or otherwise circulated in any form of binding or cover other than that in which it is published and without a similar condition including this condition being imposed on the subsequent publisher.

Lancashire, Great Britain

ISBN: 9781721111411

Contents

Prologue		7
Chapter 1	Who am I?	9
Chapter 2	My early years	11
Chapter 3	The convent	14
Chapter 4	Ken, my first husband	30
Chapter 5	The stalker	35
Chapter 6	David, my second husband	47
Chapter 7	Toy fairs	52
Chapter 8	The Lawson Street shop	58
Chapter 9	Transport Models	61
Chapter 10	Jim, my third	65
Chapter 11	The book and my customers	69
Chapter 12	Retirement	82
Chapter 13	Oyston Mill and more customers	86

PROLOGUE

I could not open my eyes. Two leather-gloved hands were holding my face. I gripped them to stop them going around my throat, as my son slept soundly next to me.

A refined voice said, 'Where is your husband?'

'I haven't got one.'

'Boyfriend?'

'No.'

The man didn't appear to have an accent, neither cigarettes nor alcohol on his breath. I kept my eyes tightly closed.

'Please do not hurt my boy,' I begged.

'Will you come to the other bedroom so I can make love to you?'

'No, I can't do that.'

The veins in my neck felt as though they were going to burst; my chest hurt with the pounding of my heart.

'I think I'm going to have a heart attack,' I gasped. 'I've already had one. Please call for an ambulance.'

'I will go if you promise not to scream again.'

'I will not scream. Thank you for not hurting us.'

This was the only time the stalker entered my house as far as I am aware. Luckily, he left without physically hurting me but afterwards I suffered with severe stress. He then stalked me for the next two years. It has left me with a fear of being in my own home unless all the door and window bolts are fully secure. If someone comes to the front door I will pretend I am not at home, even though I may know the caller. Although this happened to me some fifty years ago, the fear I felt on that night will never leave me, and the impact it had will always influence my day to day life.

1
WHO AM I?

When I read a book, especially a biography, I try to visualise the person writing it, so I will try to describe my appearance. I am eighty-three years old, quite attractive (so I am told), five feet tall (was 5' 2" but seem to have lost 2" recently!), dress in a classical fashion, navy or black suits, short blondish/greyish curly cropped hair (similar to Judy Dench with a little of Julie Walters thrown in!). I am not fat, but certainly not slim. I believe 'sturdy' is the word. Having recently had laser eye surgery, I no longer need glasses. Why I did not have this done years ago, I do not know.

At the time of writing I am co-director of a model and hobby shop in Preston, Lancashire. We both work full-time in the business and employ five staff. It is my intention to retire this year (2019). But, having tried this before, I know it is going to be difficult. If I do retire, and the rest of the staff take their usual annual holidays, the shop will not have enough cover through the year. What then?

I love my work, purchasing attic finds and secondhand items which are brought into the shop in rusty suitcases, dirty boxes and supermarket shopping bags. My work is a collector's dream. Why do I like large dirty boxes and old leather suitcases? This will be evident after reading my story.

2

MY EARLY YEARS

I was born in 1935, and at the age of three was sent to a junior school in Blackburn. My brother David, who was five, took me to school. My sister Norma was two years younger than myself. In those days, children were sent to school as young as possible. Traffic on the roads was very light as petrol was hard to find, so my mother trusted my brother to look after me. In those days I was known as Betty; my mother was Maggie, short for Margaret, and my dad, Arthur, always just Arthur. We were the Tierney family.

Prior to meeting my dad, my mother was a millworker. She lived in a terraced house with oilcloth on the table, on which permanently sat the typical bottle of milk, bag of sugar and large tea-stained mugs. The coal was kept under the stairs.

Mum vowed that her children would not inherit this life. We were destined for better things. My father's mother was an antique dealer, had beautiful lace tablecloths, china tea services and her dining table was always filled with delicacies. This is why Mum began dealing, with her mother-in-law as mentor.

We lived on a main road in Blackburn on which there was a hospital and some quite large Victorian houses interspersed with a few small, terraced houses. We had one of the latter. Mill workers rented properties in the rows of terraced houses behind. The Darwen to Blackburn trams would stop at the bottom of the road, and there was also a good bus service within minutes of our house.

I remember our home being filled with gilt-edged pictures in the hall, and highly polished mahogany furniture in the lounge, which we were forbidden to touch because our fingerprints would show. The kitchen table was always set with a china tea service with a spoon on every saucer and sugar and milk in their respective containers—bags of sugar and milk bottles were certainly not allowed anywhere near the table.

Neighbours thought we were 'posh'. They didn't know that my mother, not being able to afford real antiques, would put damaged ornaments facing the wall, so they looked perfect. They were not valuable.

In those days there was no television, and the whole family would gather to listen to the radio. For a treat, my dad would sometimes hang a white sheet on the wall and show films from a cine projector he had bought from the salerooms. We would watch anything, good or bad.

I had a childhood nickname: splutter-arse, given to me because I always had to be first at everything—the first to answer the front door bell (irrespective of whether or not I fell over the dog in my haste), the first to get the comic on a Sunday morning (*Dandy* or *Beano*), and the first to run anywhere ahead of my sister and brother. This was me (still is)—always the first, if not always the best. I should have been sent to the doctor's for hyperactivity. I could be overeager in play too. Whenever I tried to bathe one of my china dolls, either the head would come off in my hands or it quickly became legless. It was never my fault, of course, but I could be comforted with the knowledge that there were always more dolls to be had from the bags of secondhand toys that Mum kept in the garage.

As I write this story I am opening boxes in my brain that contain memories. It is said that the brain is a computer, and it seems like my memories have been stored in the archived section for too long. These childhood episodes seem to be erupting. Once I have written my book, perhaps I can delete them, never again to be written about.

3
THE CONVENT

Early on in my life I was gifted with a quick brain. My parents thought that a good private school would be beneficial, so in 1942, aged seven, I was sent to the Convent of Notre Dame—hopefully (for my mother's sake) to become a lady.

My parents introduced my sister and myself not as 'children of junk dealers' but as children whose parents were antique dealers. In fact, my mother had a secondhand stall on Blackburn Market, selling anything from corsets to shoes, and assorted bric-a-brac as came their way, including hundreds of books. So at an early age, having no television at home, we would read Charles Dickens, the Brontë sisters, Anna Sewell's *Black Beauty* and, our favourite, Enid Blyton's Famous Five.

My dad was only five feet tall, wore size four shoes, and always dressed in a shirt and tie, with jacket and his favourite trilby whenever he went out. My mother, same height, but in looks identical to myself, held her head high with an air of authority, similar to film star Bette Davies. She could make my dad cower and do as he was told. They drove an Austin Princess, a kind of poor man's Rolls Royce. Luckily the car was very large—it had to be to accommodate all the interesting items they were buying and selling, such as pianolas, mahogany boxes, old gramophones, and boxes and boxes of brilliant junk.

Although they became a common sight in later years, in the 1940s there were no charity shops, so my parents used to visit upper class areas, such as Lytham St Annes, from where they would buy unwanted items of clothing. My sister and I were always dressed immaculately. We had a wardrobe full of pretty dresses, the envy of our friends, but we never told anyone where they came from.

During these buying trips, my parents left us with ample household tasks. In anticipation of their arrival home, the living room had to be spotless, carpets vacuumed, hearth polished, and a nice roaring fire in the grate. The routine was that, on arrival home, my mother had to have a glass of sherry with her cigarette, then a cup of tea for both of them. My brother, sister and I would watch her flick the cigarette ash onto the newly polished hearth, as we waited and waited. 'Right,' she would eventually say, and we would all rush to the car to start unloading all the secondhand treasures they had found. The beautifully spotless house would be quickly filled with all sorts of boxes and bags. An area near the garage was filled with unwanted household junk while the more valuable items were placed carefully in boxes ready for resale.

My dad worked for an auctioneer in Ansdell, not far from Blackpool. He was a porter, whose duty was to get the items ready for sale. The auctioneers would empty houses of the recently deceased and put the furniture in the saleroom. Mum and Dad would then have to empty all the drawers in the furniture and put this into boxes, making sure there were no bank books or money. They then bought these boxes of assorted items from the auctioneers. My mum would tell me what, if anything, was collectible, such as cloisonné, for which I have had a liking ever since, together with blue and white Chinese ornaments. However, most of the antiques that came into their possession were sold on to collectors in order to cover the fees at the convent. To this day some very old items still make my hands tingle.

There was one regular antique collector who owned a sweet shop on the main road in Blackburn. We were given the task of taking him any nice pieces of pottery that my mother knew he liked. He would always invite us into his large terraced house, which had beautiful glass cupboards filled with items from Worcester and Staffordshire. When he opened the door to the cabinets, the whole room would be filled with the smell of potpourri. These cupboards also contained boxes and boxes of sweets. We would usually go home with a pocket full of fruit salad or jelly babies.

It was always easy to find the secondhand stall my parents ran on Blackburn Market because of the crowds that would gather early to see their latest offerings. My mum would know the regular customers by name, what they collected, and their dress sizes. Good quality clothing at the right price was hard to find during wartime, but they knew that she would look after them. Postcards would be handed to one collector, medals to another, tinplate toys and hard to find pottery to other collectors, of which there were many.

There was an art in checking worn garments, even though sometimes they did not smell so sweet. The hemlines had to be felt in case money had fallen through the pockets, and lapels and collars felt for broaches. The buttons on military jackets were cut off and put into bags to be sold separately. Old mahogany workboxes where ladies kept their bobbins of cotton were closely examined in case a ring or two, perhaps with the stones missing, had fallen under all the embroidery silks. These were placed in bags—one for silver, one for gold. Good cutlery was usually Electro Plated Nickel Silver (EPNS) which, when polished, would enhance any dining table. Polishing was one of our jobs, so the knives, forks, spoons and other such items would sell for more money. Now and again we would find a solid silver spoon, but this was a rare occurrence.

One great piece of advice given to me by my mother was, 'Buy for one penny and sell for one and a half pennies. If you try to get two pence and it is not worth it, you will never get rich. If you sell for one and a half pennies, and you do this every day, you could be a millionaire in time.'

When I first went to the convent school, due to the brilliant recommendations from my previous teachers, I was placed in a class a year above my age group. However, the convent girls, some boarders, some day boarders, and the other day pupils, had already started learning algebra, fractions and geometry. I was absolutely clueless, and from that day I have never found out how $b - c = d$. I was ridiculed because of my lack of maths abilities (and I thought I was ugly because it seemed no one liked me, but that's another story). It was only later in life that someone showed me how to calculate fractions by using oranges. I finally understood how to halve a sixteenth. I never did any homework, but I had a photographic memory. I could read a chapter of a book or poem on my way to school, and repeat it verbatim soon after, but two days later I would have forgotten it completely.

To earn pocket money we would make toys out of bits and pieces of wool we found in the junk boxes. I used to make little dolls by winding black wool around my hands, tying a piece of thicker wool around to make a waist, dividing it to make the legs, and threading more wood through the body to make two arms. Then I would put a face on and add yellow tufts of hair, and sit on my front doorstep and sell them to the American soldiers who were convalescing in the infirmary opposite. My sister Norma and I would ask the neighbours for magazines for the soldiers (making sure there were no 'naughty' pictures in them before being sent across the road). I once confessed to our priest that we had seen these pictures before tearing them out. He just smiled.

Food was in short supply. Everyone was given a ration book containing coupons, and a wartime number that we had to memorise. I can still recall mine: NBOA 72 4. Rationing meant long queues at the shops, especially the butcher's. I remember queueing for about an hour to buy sausages from a shop a mile from our house. The distance walked and the effort expended to get the sausages meant they were absolutely delicious, or at least seemed like it, even though we were only allowed one each. Sweets were also rationed; so much so that I would walk three miles to school to save my bus fare so that I could buy a penny bag of broken chocolate pieces or biscuits from Woolworth's. There were no obese children in those days.

My mother would get a chicken from one of her farmer friends, simmer it for hours, take out all the bones, press the chicken and make an enormous pan full of soup from the jellied gravy. She would then take bottles of the soup to the market for other stallholders and farming customers who, in turn, would give her eggs, butter and bacon. One way or another we were always well fed. The cold chicken would be sliced, together with the jelly that had formed around it, and served with homemade bread.

From time to time we played with the children in the streets behind our house. Norma and I would exchange our leather shoes for a pair of their clogs when we were playing out, as they had metal tips which, if you quickly scraped your foot on the ground, would create sparks. Now, my mother was spending a lot of money to transform us into ladies, and it was certainly not right for any convent girl to be found wearing clogs, especially not the workers' black ones. She decided enough was enough and bought us both a pair of rubber-soled clogs—my sister's green with red a pattern; mine red with green. She had not grasped the significance of why we wanted the black clogs. The big attraction was the metal tips. The rubber-soled clogs were never worn.

From beginning to end I hated my days at the convent. There were many reasons. I detested the trips every Friday to the chapel, walking with head bowed, hands together in prayer, and the singing of hymns. In later life, people have told me that, as far as eating is concerned, I am eccentric—I blame the school and the nuns for my behaviour. Every lunchtime we would have to walk in single file across the main road, then across a wooden bridge over a small river to the refectory. Remaining in single file, we would enter the wooden building, which resembled a scout hut. We sat at long wooden tables with benches on each side and a chair at the head of each table on which sat a nun in her usual black and white habit with a large cross around her neck. We never saw the hair, and speculated that it may have been shaved off. We were not allowed to speak.

Soup first. We could not begin eating until every girl was served. We had to wait until the silent nun lifted her downcast eyes, surveyed us, then slowly nodded her head. Eating the soup had to adhere to certain formalities. The plate had to be tilted backwards so the soup tilted away, not towards, you. The spoon had to be placed in the soup without touching the bowl, then raised to the mouth and—quietly—sipped and swallowed. That was just the soup course. We still had the main course and pudding to look forward to! The room was eerily quiet, not a clatter of spoons or a swallow could be heard. If a girl so much as touched the plate with her cutlery, she would be sent to face the wall in shame.

This strict mealtime regime left me with certain food foibles that people find difficult to understand. For instance, I feel sick if I see someone eating with their mouth open. If they make a noise at all, whether with their knives, forks or spoons, I glower at them and, as for eating an apple, this is forbidden within earshot. To me, the crunching of boiled sweets and crisps is a crime. Whenever I visit friends in their homes and they ask me to join them for a meal, I have to graciously decline. What's worse is that my children have inherited my intolerances. I know there are other individuals who are similar, but I am definitely classed as odd.

I never really reached my potential at the convent until it came to the Eleven Plus examination. As I was only ten, I was allowed to sit the exam with the proviso that, if I failed, I could resit the following year. I passed first time. I was offered a place at the 'big' school (still a year younger than my classmates) with no more fees to pay. As I was always top in art and music, I remained level pegging with most of the others in my new class. There were three streams: Latin, for the cleverest, then German, followed by the bottom level for the remaining girls who, like myself, seemed to flounder. I was no better at sport. There was a netball team with the usual three or four reserves. I was always the last reserve. But I made up for it by being good at gymnastics—I could climb a rope like a monkey. Even though I hated the days at this school, I can never thank my mother enough for sending me there. I am always proud to say that I was a Convent of Notre Dame Grammar schoolgirl.

I learned to read music and play the piano, but always found the left hand parts more difficult than playing the melody with the right. I always passed the obligatory examinations, albeit with low marks. I could listen to a melody, write the music down and readily play it back. Then I had to sing. I always seemed to sing the notes I had written, but apparently the noise coming from my mouth did not resemble in any shape or form the original version. No matter how hard I tried, I could not do this. How can you improve if you already think you are singing in tune? I could tell which scale was being played, but I could not sing it, and I don't think I will ever be able to. I have always said that if I am ever born again I will ask God if I can be a singer, slightly taller, and with nice white teeth. It is not asking for much.

I also enjoyed art classes. I was the teacher's pet (most of the other teachers were nuns and I was never a pet of any nun), so I was nearly always the top in art. I could draw a person standing or sitting, and copy pictures, and I loved mixing colours. Because many other girls were boarders, they became pets of the nuns, but I did not fit into this bracket. Many of their parents were military personnel who lived abroad and entrusted the nuns with the care of their children. If they wanted them to be taught in a strict environment, these children were in good hands; the rules were very, very strict.

One example was our appearance. We had to walk down the road in twos, not threes or fours, but twos. Our summer panama hats had to be placed at the correct angle, we always had to wear gloves, our skirts had to be level with the knee, and socks and shoes worn as laid down in the rules and regulations.

Often I have questioned whether I could have been proficient in maths if I had been put in the correct class. Would I have been clever enough to go to Oxford or Cambridge? If so, I would certainly not be in a Preston model shop at the age of eighty-three selling toy trains. I could have been a professor, retiring at, say, fifty-five with a fantastic pension and a flat in Tenerife.

From an early age my brother David went to a Jesuit college in Grange-over-Sands as his ambition was to be a priest. As a youngster he had an altar in his bedroom. He didn't play out like most children, and my mother thought he was going to be the next saint because he was born on December 21. He left college at sixteen and attended another college in France. However, he returned home with a changed attitude towards the church. He told my mother that all priests were evil, and he never went to church again. Nothing was said at the time, but events in recent years have made me question whether or not he was one of those children who were abused by Catholic priests. He helped my dad when he was home from school and, being six feet tall with black hair, customers called them Steptoe and Son. We didn't have a horse and cart, but they certainly fitted the description. He later left home and joined the merchant navy.

I loved my dad and his naive approach to life. I can illustrate it with an incident that happened at C&A, the big department store. Because my parents were secondhand dealers, we never had new clothes. However, one day my mum and dad decided to have an afternoon out in the new department store. I wanted a new dress—anything but green, as this was the colour of my school uniform—and my sister too. After searching for two long hours, I finally ended up with... a green one. In the meantime my mother insisted that my dad buy a pair of shoes, much to his disgust. He went off to buy the shoes and we all went home. On the Sunday, Mum told Dad to wear his new shoes. Again, he did what Mum told him to do. After about an hour he started limping.

'What are you limping for?' she asked.

'The shoes hurt. The left one is all right; it is the right one.'

Mum told him to take them off so she could inspect the inside.

'Arthur,' she said, 'these are two odd shoes.'

'But they're both lace-ups,' he said.

'Arthur,' she said with more emphasis, 'you have one brown shoe and one black. And I know why this one is hurting; it has a compass in the heel.'

Because he only took size four shoes, my dad had gone to the boys' section at C&A and left the store with a single junior Pathfinder shoe.

Then my mum became pregnant and had a little boy. I hated this baby. I was at the age when I could meet my friends on a Saturday afternoon in town but, because my mum had to work and go to her stall on the market, I would be left in charge of this spoilt, unhealthy infant. He was always ill because he suffered with asthma. Norma had dancing lessons and my brother David was in the shop with my dad, so I got no help from them.

My mother always tried her best to send us to as many extracurricular lessons as possible. My sister and I were sent to ballet and tap dancing classes. Norma was excellent from the outset; she could easily point her toes, but of course I could not manage it. I soon left. Next, I went for ballroom dancing lessons to see if that suited me better. Classes were held in a large house on Preston New Road. One of the girls in the class was called Elaine, an attractive girl with beautiful blonde hair. There were other girls with brassy blonde hair, a colour my mother always called 'common', so I didn't want to go this colour. My hair at that time was curly and very mousey. I asked Elaine how to get my hair the same colour as hers. She told me her secret: Macleans dental peroxide. She said that if I put a few drops in with my shampoo, the hair will slowly lighten. I bought the peroxide at the chemist and some Sta-Blonde shampoo at Woolworths. Gradually my hair went lighter, and my mother would comment every week that my hair looked blonder. I lied. I showed her the bottle of shampoo, which stated that it made blonde hair look brighter.

My grandmother lived in a house on one of the streets behind our home, which had also been where my mother had been brought up (the one with the store of coal underneath the stairs). She used to sit in her rocking chair so close to the fire that the skin on her legs was always highly patterned bright red. I wondered why she didn't have a bust, or didn't appear to, but I later found out that this was because her boobs hung down to her waist. She always wore an apron, toasted her bread over the black iron grates of an open fire, and slurped tea from an enormous cup at the same time as having a slice of bread in her mouth. My grandfather lived in a shop near the convent but, as he had left my grandmother and married another woman, it was frowned upon to visit him. Now and again when Norma and I visited his shop, he would give us money—not a shilling or half a crown, but a £5 note each. I can remember quite distinctly asking him what I might do if I were to work for myself. His advice was to always work at something you are good at and you enjoy, and you will succeed. My life didn't quite work out that way.

When I was about seventeen, my father opened an antique shop on Bolton Road in Blackburn. Seven years later, in around 1959, he moved to another shop at the top of King Street. Buying and selling must be in the blood.

Just before I left school I became friends with a grammar school girl called Mavis. I envied her from the day we met. She had straight, naturally white hair, was the same height as myself, and was always beautifully tanned. As soon as the sun came out, she would look upwards and her body would change colour. She had perfectly shaped legs, tiny feet and thin ankles. She could play piano—with both hands, not just one—and at the same time sing along with the music and, strangely, never asked me to join in. Every boy we met would turn to look at her. She went to university and came home with a degree. In later life she married, had two children, and became the headmistress of her local school. She died over thirty years ago, so I suppose I didn't really envy her after all.

I left school with one O level and passed the examination for religion with distinction plus... then went to work in a mill office. My first wage was almost £2, and my mum made an agreement with me that she would take £1 for board and lodgings, and I could have the remaining nineteen shillings, barely enough to buy clothes and make-up. The price of a pair of nylon stockings was ten shillings, which left just nine shillings to cover bus fares and anything else I needed. For the next three years I changed jobs regularly while attending night school three nights a week for shorthand and typing, and finally ended up as a secretary. My mother was very proud as I was now what she termed 'a lady'. The various jobs I had as a teenager helped a great deal in later life because I learned bookkeeping, cashier work and maths, including fractions, percentages and especially adding up columns and columns of figures. (Luckily it wasn't necessary to know algebra or geometry.) There were no mechanical aids in those days. All had to be done in the head, so to speak, so now I can add up pages and pages of figures in my head quicker than a calculator.

There were two dance halls in Blackburn: one, King George's Hall, often frequented by convent girls, high school girls, and boys from their respective grammar schools; the second was called Tony's. I was never allowed to go to this venue because of the supposedly unsavoury characters who went there. Well, my mother said they were unsavoury. I met a boy in King George's Hall one Saturday night. He was six feet, handsome in his own way, and eventually we became engaged and then married. Because I was generally at night school during the week, the weekends were the only times we got together. Rock and Roll music was all the rage at the time and the girls wore the usual full skirts with masses and masses of frills underneath, tight, black elastic belt at the waist, and white patterned blouses. The nylon stockings we wore were normally decorated with black patterns down the side of the legs, and very high-heeled shoes were in fashion. On odd occasions we went by train to Blackpool to dance in the Tower Ballroom, but always had to catch the last train home.

I have not written a great deal about my sister Norma. However, one weekend my mother insisted I took her to the Tower Ballroom. Norma was certainly not as 'advanced' as I was. She was, of course, two years younger than myself, which then would make her fourteen. As far as I was concerned, she was a child. I had the task of making her look a little older, but Norma would not co-operate. Norma would not wear the usual flimsy silk suspender belt, but adamantly insisted on wearing her 'liberty bodice' with the suspenders stitched on the bottom. She was certainly not slim, but quite rounded, and that day wore her best frilly dress which made her appear more rounded.

Beautiful blonde Mavis and I, together with my sister, got off the train in Blackpool and walked to the Tower Ballroom, stood on the perimeter of the dance floor waiting to be asked to dance. Who should be asked to dance first, but Norma, and this carried on all night. The boys crowded around, and Mavis and I were certainly pushed to one side.

It was around this time my parents bought their first television. My dad could never understand how my mother could go into three shops to look for cheap nylons, and return to the car having ordered a television on the 'never never'. As we were the only family in our road who owned a television, my mother invited as many people as would fit into our house to watch the Queen's Coronation.

Aged seventeen, I was quite ignorant of the reproductive principals. The nuns never spoke about such topics, and my mother would not allow any of us to hold hands with the opposite sex in front of her. As we left the house to go dancing, my grandmother would say, 'It only takes a minute for a lifetime of unhappiness.' I had no idea what she was talking about, so completely ignored her. It was left, therefore, to my boyfriend to tell me what happened, how and why, as we experimented. Such revelations.

4
KEN, MY FIRST HUSBAND

My husband and I were lucky enough to buy a new house for £3,000. Because we were both employed, it was easy to get a mortgage. We had only been married about six months when we had our first major row. I had been brought up in a house where there were no rows: Mum said this; Dad did that. When Ken and I moved into our newly built house, we had an electric fire fitted in the bedroom and plastered in situ. One chilly morning I put the fire on to get dressed. My husband said it was warm enough without the fire and switched it off. I switched it back on. This happened a few times. In the end I took hold of the fire, and told him that, if I can't have it on, then I didn't need it, and pulled it off the wall. Unfortunately, half the wall came with it. My husband stormed out of the house. I then left for work, where I cried all day, eventually developing a migraine, and had to go home. At home I looked for painkillers, but could only find one aspirin and one Cephos powder. I took both and went to bed, leaving the empty packets on the kitchen table. I woke up with my husband and the next door neighbours shaking me, asking how many tablets I had taken. They thought

I had attempted suicide. I have never in my life wanted to end it, and never will.

After two years of marriage I became pregnant and had my first daughter. Six months later my mother-in-law offered to look after her so that I could go back to work. I had put on a lot of weight having the baby, and my husband's nickname for me was 'Michelin tyre lady'. He did not mince his words and could be quite cruel at times. Perhaps it was time to lose a few pounds. A weightlifter opened a ladies exercise class in a rundown room in Blackburn town centre. My neighbours and I joined and, after about six months, three of us decided we would like to try lifting weights. Within a year we could do the clean and jerk, press, snatch, and other competition lifts. A TV presenter covering the north of England came to interview three of us and we appeared on television—my one and only claim to fame.

I decided to change jobs and had an interview to be a receptionist in a large engineering company. I got the job and was soon promoted to secretary to the managing director, where I stayed for about six years. After my second daughter was born, the director set up his own engineering company and asked if I would do his secretarial work from home. I didn't even have the necessary equipment, such as a typewriter and duplicating machine. I thought that if he wanted me to do secretarial work, there must be other people who wanted the same, so I rented an office on Richmond Terrace in Blackburn. Most of the offices on this terrace were occupied by solicitors and accountants. With a £300 loan and one typewriter, I formed Elizabeth French Limited. After twelve months, just as I was attracting new customers, I became pregnant again. As the time drew closer to having the baby, I took on my first employee, Joan. It was a bad time to take leave from the business, so I couldn't let the birth of a child affect the fledgling business. I was at work on the Tuesday, had my son the following day, and was back at work on the Sunday.

The business expanded and I persuaded my husband to sell our new detached home in Wilpshire and buy an old Victorian house on the main road in Blackburn. This large house had ornate rooms on the ground floor that could accommodate the office stationery and furniture side of the business. There were car parks to the front and rear of the building, and we had a flat on the first and second floors. It was perfect. When the business expanded further my husband came to work with me and took over the printing while I continued with the secretarial and office equipment supplies. The business grew until we employed about ten staff. In order to develop the print side of the business I tried to attend technical college to learn how to use a Multilith duplicating machine, camera and guillotine. I went for the first lesson. The printing union heard of my attendance, requested I leave, and instructed the college that if I ever returned they would withdraw all their labour from the college. This was at a time when the unions held power, but not over me. We still printed our leaflets, but could not produce booklets, as the other printers in the area were banned from finishing my work.

I had purchased the house in Blackburn from a man who in later years became a director of a professional football club. He leased a very small island in the Pacific called Anegada and it was his intention to create a miniature Bahamas. In fact, it was the northernmost island of the British Virgin Islands. He asked me to print the brochures and leaflets for his new venture, then invited me to go out and live on the island and set up the secretarial and office administration side, as there was nothing in operation in these early days. He gave me the name of his accountants and asked me to telephone them for further details. They told me that my children would have to live on a neighbouring island so they could go to school. With that information I decided that they were too young for so much upset and declined the offer. I understand this is now a beautiful island with lots of hotels, golf courses and other holiday amenities, but the island suffered badly from recent tropical storms.

Meanwhile, my husband spent a lot of his time playing golf, so most weekends he would be on the course. Ken always found time to do what he wanted to do, irrespective of family life. His mood on Sunday evenings depended on whether or not he had played well. We either all suffered from his anger or the night was relatively peaceful.

But I was not happy, in fact I was quite deeply depressed. I had been seeing the doctor for some time because I cried a lot. I could not find any solution to my problems and I couldn't take my husband's outbursts anymore, so I offered him a lump sum if he would give me a divorce. With the money I gave him, he bought his own flat and set up a printing business in opposition.

I then purchased a bungalow on the outskirts of Blackburn, near the cemetery, and moved there with the two girls. Ken would not let me take our son as he adored him but, because he was not well, he later allowed our son to come live with us.

5
THE STALKER

Within a year after separating from my first husband, my children had settled into our new home. My elder daughter had by now got a boyfriend. After returning from a party one night, the boyfriend told me I was being watched. He said that when he had pulled up at my door, about 10 p.m., there had been an unfamiliar car parked two houses down. The driver came alongside their window, took a long hard look at the passengers, then drove off. I didn't think anything about it at the time.

Later that year I took my younger daughter, then aged about eight, and my son, six, to a New Year's Eve party. Just before leaving, I thought I heard someone come into the house. The children looked into the various rooms, but did not go into my bedroom, which was in an extension on the ground floor. The party was only a family affair and, when ready to leave at the end of the evening, the hostess asked me if my daughter could stay the night with her daughter, who was the same age. Unfortunately their son already had a friend staying, which left my very tearful son to come home with me. When we arrived back in the house I told him that I would get into bed with him and we could both have a special breakfast in bed the following morning. With that he fell asleep.

At this point I should describe my home. It was a dormer bungalow with a bay window on each side of the front door. I slept in the ground floor extension at the back of the house, my son was in a small bedroom next to mine, and my two daughters slept in the dormer bedrooms. At the back of the house was a dining room with French windows, which I used as a second lounge. I did not have any curtains as my back garden was very private and, as I thought at the time, not easily accessible to any public. On the other side of this second lounge was a small kitchen with a back door. There was a driveway down one side of the house, which led to a seventy-five foot-long back garden. At the bottom there was a steep drop into the park below.

Back to New Year's Eve. My son and I were both asleep in the shared bed. I was awakened by something touching my face. I sensed someone in the room and tried to scream. I clutched two leather-gloved hands to stop them from going around my throat.

'Where is your husband?' asked the voice.

'I haven't got one.'

'Boyfriend?'

'No.'

'I have been watching you and I like you. I am six feet, twenty-five and not ugly. Will you be my girlfriend?'

All I kept repeating was, 'Please do not hurt my boy.'

There is no way to describe the pounding of my heart, and the vessels in my neck that felt like they were going to burst.

'Will you come into the bedroom so I can make love to you?' he said.

His breath did not smell of alcohol or cigarettes. I never opened my eyes, kept them tightly shut.

'No.'

I then said, 'Please send for an ambulance. I am going to have a heart attack. I have had one before.'

I couldn't breathe and my chest hurt so much.

He said he would leave, providing I did not scream.

'I will not scream.'

I thanked him for not hurting me and my boy.

With that, he left the room. It was then that I opened my eyes and looked as he went out of the room. I noticed as he left that he was wide and reached the top of the door jamb, and seemed to walk from side to side as though he had a limp. As soon as he left I jumped out of bed, pushed the wardrobe between the bed and the door, opened the bedroom window and screamed for my neighbours. Eventually they came and sent for the police. They of course assumed that I had gone to the party and invited someone back to the house. I informed the police that men were not allowed in the house without other people being present, and my children knew all the people that came. The police took the children to one side, who of course confirmed everything I had said.

A week later someone tried to get into the house, but by then I had fitted extra door locks. Whoever it was soon left. Of course

I informed the police. This became a regular, weekly occurrence for about twelve months. I was not the only one to hear the doors being tried. Police took plaster casts from footprints in the garden and footprints in the snow made in the middle of the night, but they did nothing. Actually they insinuated that perhaps I had someone make the footprints so that they would believe me.

I had better explain at this point the difficulty that police had in keeping watch on my house. My road was an offshoot to the cemetery. There was an old people's home on one side, with grass all around, houses, including mine, on the right-hand side, and in front, past three more detached bungalows, were two large gates, which gave entry to the cemetery. To get to the back of my house you could either go down my drive or drive down the road, through these gates into the cemetery, and turn right down another small road. To get into my back garden an intruder would have to climb up a rather steep hillock, generally on all fours, making it virtually impossible for anyone to catch the stalker. The peeping tom would go through the park at the back of the house, climb the hill, then cross my garden to get to my back door. Every time I telephoned the police for assistance, they would come down the road in the police car as the stalker ran into the park. The police soon became sceptical of my complaints. In fact, they didn't believe there was a stalker at all. I became a talking point at the station —I was the mad woman with the children. After quite a few phone calls I asked if an officer could be put on watch. The reply from the person at the station was: 'You pay the same rates as everyone else; it's not possible.' Ultimately I had floor to ceiling curtains fitted in the back lounge.

One night I walked from my living room into the kitchen and noticed a shadow at the bottom of the garden, which disappeared behind a tree. I turned the light off and looked out of the window. I waited for about half an hour, not taking my eyes off the tree. I then decided enough was enough, I was not going to send for the police again, closed the curtains, and carried on polishing the brasses in the hearth. I felt so tired that I lay on the floor, duster in hand, and must have fallen asleep. I woke to the sound of people in my garden. I pulled back the floor to ceiling curtains to see the back garden filled with police. I asked what had happened. A police sergeant who lived in a bungalow two houses down, said that, on returning from night duty, he found his dustbin under the window of his house.

'Did you hear anything?' he asked.

'Yes,' I said. 'If you look behind that tree you will see his footprints. He was there for about half an hour.'

'Why did you not telephone us?'

'But you never do anything, do you?'

The police took plaster casts of the footprints and told me that whoever it was wore wellingtons.

I relayed all this to my neighbour who gasped, and said, 'There is a man who always wears wellingtons and walks across the green. He has a white chow dog. He always makes a point of looking into your house.'

She told this to the police, who went to find the man with the dog, and took him down to the police station. The following day

I was in the front lounge with my children when I saw a man walking across the green with the white chow. I told the children that if he came to the house, they had to stay by my side and not to leave me on my own. The man knocked, and I went to the door, a child on each side of me.

'Hello, Betty,' he said.

I recognised him. The man in front of me was called Harry. I used to play with him and his brother as a child in the infirmary grounds opposite my house.

'I thought it was you,' he said. 'I have been looking out to see if I could see you.'

His presence seemed innocent enough and he was ruled out as a suspect.

My health deteriorated. I could not sleep at night, so one of my staff from work would bring tasks to do at my home and I would sleep for part of the day. I was a frequent visitor at the doctor's surgery, but he was at a loss how to help me. He then suggested a psychiatrist. He made an appointment for me to attend a private clinic and, on entering, the psychiatrist's first words were, 'Do you know I only accept cash.' I went for about six sessions, but most of the time he complained about his own problems, yet still wanted payment.

One night around 11 p.m. in early August, six months following my attack, I heard a noise outside once more. I was still having trouble sleeping. I looked through the front window and saw a man on all fours beneath the window looking up at me. He soon ran off. Of course I informed the police and was taken to the station to study photographs of known criminals in the area, but to no avail. I then telephoned the psychiatrist and told him that I would never improve in health unless the stalker was caught, and I never attended again.

Then came my birthday, August 10. I had a small party for my children and their friends from next door. As it was getting dark I realised that I had forgotten to take our white highland terrier out for his usual walk. I would usually never do this by myself at that time of night. I told the children to keep a watch on me as I went over the road with the dog and his favourite toy. I threw the toy back and forth, giving the dog plenty of exercise. On one occasion the toy landed near a bush. As I bent down to pick it up, I saw a pair of very shiny brown leather shoes. I didn't stop to see who was wearing them so I quickly picked up the toy, threw it towards my house then ran across the road and through my front door, closing it behind me. I had promised my neighbour earlier that I would not mention the intruder to her children, so I didn't say anything as they were staying the night. Not long after going to bed, my neighbour's daughter ran into the lounge in hysterics saying she heard someone outside who was apparently trying to get in through the front door.

Two or three days later I heard noises in the garden, and my dog was having hysterics at the French window. I again rang for the police. A very young policeman came. As he had not been to my house before and was ignorant of the stalker history, I told him of my difficulties. We had been talking for about ten minutes when we both heard a scraping sound. He jumped up.

'I heard that,' he said.

He then shouted and ran through the back door into the garden. I heard him shout again, then nothing. All was quiet. He did not return. I waited so long that I had to telephone the police again. I explained that I was worried for the policeman.

The man on the line shouted, 'Stay where you are and don't go out. Someone has been spotted.'

Later I heard the pounding of feet around the house and I tried to see what was happening through the window. There was nothing. The police went away and I was left in my home, not knowing whether to go to bed or stay up. Had they caught my stalker? After another hour I telephoned the police again who said everything was now okay and I should go to bed.

Some time after this episode, one of my staff telephoned me to say there was a man in my showroom who wanted some furniture because he was setting up an office. He said he was going to be a private detective. Thinking he could possibly do some work for me, I went in to work to meet him.

He was an impressive six feet tall and very well-dressed. We talked for a while as I explained my situation. He said he would be delighted to help, and asked if he could wait at my office for his wife to turn up. Ten minutes later a little woman, about four feet eight, arrived with long, stringy black, unkempt hair, an enormous bust, and two protruding front teeth. Surely this was not his wife. However, it was.

I took both of them to my house. I remember it was a Friday because that was chicken night. It was routine.

'Oh John, what a good smell,' she said.

'We haven't had chicken for a long time,' he replied.

I sat them on the settee, then the children came home from school.

John got out a box of tobacco and a cigarette rolling machine, and pulled some old dog ends to pieces so he could roll another cigarette.

'Would you like one of my cigarettes?' I asked.

'Oh John,' she said, 'proper cigarettes. We can't afford these.'

I made them coffees and chicken sandwiches.

It was arranged that I would pick them up the following afternoon from the other side of Blackburn and bring them again to my home. After we had drunk our first cup of coffee, John left the house to have a look around the area. I told him that, should we have a problem at the house, I would switch the light on in the unused front room, signaling him to return. After he left, his wife took the cups into the kitchen, and John mistook this light to be a signal. He must have run to the back of the house. With the noise from the back garden, the dog started jumping at the window, and his wife started screaming that she had heard noises. I opened the French doors, and in the dusk was the outline of a man. It was John.

After another cup of coffee I asked him how he had become a detective and how many years experience he had with the police. 'None,' he said. His wife went on to say that when the April fair came to Blackburn, as it did every year, they visited a fortune teller who told them that John would either become a film star or a private detective, so he chose the latter.

In the meantime he had obtained a position as a night porter at a very good hotel in Blackburn that had provided him with the suit he was in today as a uniform. I thanked them for their help and gave them a small amount of money, which was probably a fortune to them, and they left.

One night in November I had to go to my business premises. A friend of mine, a coach driver, said he would babysit the children for an hour. I could not ask my neighbour as she was more frightened than I was. On the way home it started to snow. The coach driver (I have forgotten his name) opened the back door, made me a coffee and said he would have to leave as he had an early start the following morning. As he was about to go he heard a noise from outside the door.

'I heard that,' he said, and opened the back door.

There were footprints from the end of the garden to the back door and back again to the park. He telephoned the police. They came and insinuated that my friend had made the footprints so that they would believe my stories about being stalked.

I lost my cool, and said, 'I will catch him if you won't.'

I ran from the kitchen, got into the car, reversed out of the drive and down the road. I drove through the park gates and took the road that led behind my house. The car stalled and I could not start it again, so there I was, in the dark, in the park, no car and I had to climb the hill at the back of my house to get home. Something flew out of the bushes in front of me, and by the time I arrived back inside the house I could hardly breathe through fright.

During this time my bungalow was up for sale. It was on the market for about a year. It was a really difficult time. The mortgage interest rate was about 14%, so the property market was stagnant. Because of my continuing loss of weight, no doubt partially due to the weekly visits from the stalker, one of my staff offered to live in the company flat with me, so I left the house empty and moved back into Preston New Road. Needless to say the nightmarish conditions continued, but this time it was my employee and friend who answered the nightly silent telephone calls and called the police if anything untoward happened.

I couldn't sleep, and did not return to work for about a year. My weight dropped to five stone. The business suffered. I finally took the accountant's advice and put the company into voluntary liquidation. By this time, the 1970s, the three-day week had made trading conditions difficult for any business. I didn't have the strength to fight the fight because of the fear of my unknown stalker. I lost the business.

The last time I heard or worried about this person was when I had to go to the children's school for a prize-giving night. My daughter was going to receive an award for the child who had tried the hardest. I asked two boys from a Nigerian family who lived opposite to stay in with my son. The younger of the two brothers played with my son in the evenings and at weekends. When I arrived back home about nine o'clock the sixteen-year-old boy asked me if I knew I was being watched. He said he had seen someone across the road in some bushes watching my flat for about an hour. He didn't know whether or not to call the police. He knew nothing about my stalker. I asked him if he could see what the man looked like. All he said was that he was a big man who appeared to have a limp. I never saw or heard the stalker again.

Not long after, I had to vacate the flat in Blackburn and I returned to my unsold bungalow. My business was in liquidation and the business property had been auctioned and sold. I was offered work with a printers and stationers in Burnley and continued in employment with them for about two years. Then I met David.

6
DAVID, MY SECOND HUSBAND

I met David at a friend's silver wedding party three years after my divorce from Ken. There was an instant attraction, even though he was twelve years my junior. He told me that he had just split from someone and was presently living with a friend. He resembled George from the George and Mildred sitcom, which, admittedly, is not a flattering description, but quite accurate. He was working as a heavy haulage driver and, after a few weeks, I decided that, since he had no real home, he could move in with me and my children. He arrived one night with just a bag of wet washing fresh from the launderette and a few dry clothes in another bag. I really should have sensed that it was wrong for a person of his age to have nothing of value, other than a bag of wet washing.

While we were getting to know each other, I received an offer for the house, so David and I discussed a move to a better part of the country. We decided Torquay would be a nice place to live and bring up the children. Soon it was Easter and I had holidays from work and, thinking David was on holiday too, drove down to the south coast to have a look at flats and consider our prospects. We arrived home to find that David had been sacked from his job as he had taken leave of absence without permission. He applied for another job with a local haulage company, but after two weeks broke his arm and could not work for another ten weeks. The same day he had the plaster taken off, he was playing with my son, who was trying some Kung Fu moves. He kicked David unintentionally and broke his other arm, so he was off work again for another ten weeks.

In the meantime I had been introduced to David's family. He had a son and daughter and had been estranged from his mother for some time. I could not understand this, so I forced him to invite her to my home so that he could patch up his differences. She took me to one side and asked me quite candidly why I liked her son. I acknowledged that he never appeared to be happy. She laughed. I said he reminded me of Victor Meldrew, the grumpy sitcom character.

'Victor Meldrew,' she scoffed. 'David is ten times worse than him. Victor Meldrew is quite happy compared to David.'

At the time I thought this was a little harsh.

By now my home had been sold, so we moved to Torquay. It was a disaster. David could not find a job and eventually we returned to St Annes-on-Sea. He began to work on the taxis and I found employment with the Official Receiver in bankruptcy as a typist. Because I was in secure employment, we arranged a mortgage on a large terraced house. We redecorated, took down walls, and made the place our own.

By this time I realised it was more or less impossible to please David, however hard I tried. He ate nothing but beef, and would not let me cook any other meat. The smell of chicken made him sick, so I could only cook it if he was not in the house, and I had to open all doors and windows afterwards. We had steak, minced beef, stewed steak, beef burgers, beef sausage, anything that had the word beef in it. Occasionally he would try pork chops, but always complained afterwards. It was beef, beef, beef.

After two years in this house he decided it would be nicer to live nearer the sea, so that's what we did, again in St Annes. David was not still not happy. He applied for work once more as a driver, but the money was poor, so he worked on alternate days and nights, which understandably interfered with his metabolism. He then transferred to working long distance, which meant he was away from home most days. He was never satisfied.

We then went to see his sister who had a smallholding in Wales. It was a beautiful day—the farm pig had just had piglets, two donkeys ambled around a field, and flowers surrounded the house. On a whim David decided this was the life for him. No more days away from home on the road. We sold our house, ready for a move to Wales.

We signed the house sale contracts when my daughter, unmarried, told me she was pregnant, which made it difficult for me to go to Wales until her baby was born. David went on his own to find us a house. He found a very small bungalow in the middle of a hill with a stream running around it. It had a smallholding reference, which was important because he wanted to breed pigs. We moved in after the birth of my granddaughter, and I got a position as secretary to the Chief Medical Officer for Wales. Unfortunately the smallholding licence had expired and the council would not renew it, as some new houses had been built opposite our land, and they did not want the smell of pigs to spoil the area.

David had no job. He tried in vain to gain employment, but because we only had one car and the village had hardly any bus service, the prospects looked bleak. It was unfortunate because Wales is a very poor country and the Welsh community prefer Welsh speaking locals. However, eventually he was offered a job during the potato season, which meant I had to get up at 4 a.m., drive him to the other side of Wales so he could pick up the lorry to deliver the potatoes, then return to pick him up at the end of the day.

The job was seasonal, so after being out of work again for some months, David decided to move back to St Annes and get a job on the taxis. He said he would drive down to Wales when possible. To be very truthful, I welcomed this arrangement with open arms. Our relationship was not working. Even the doctor I worked for told me how happy I appeared to be after David left. I promised faithfully I would look after his ducks and hens, but after he had gone and I had fed these creatures for a few early mornings in the rain and wind before work, a friend told me she would take them and put them with hers on a farm. That was one less thing to worry about.

I stayed in Carmarthen for another year with David working in St Annes and coming down at weekends. Eventually, after visiting the local supermarket and studying which tinned stewed steak—beef again—was the cheapest, I knew the end had come. Was this what my life had come to? I gave my notice at work and moved back to Lancashire. I then lived with my daughter in Longridge for about six months, refusing to see David, but eventually I gave in and decided to try again. I got a job with the Crown Prosecution Service in Preston and David went to work for a tyre company, but this was hard, dirty work, certainly not what he wanted.

This time we bought a house in Preston, even though we didn't have enough money left over from the move for furniture and curtains. To raise a bit of extra cash, it was decided that David would sell his model railways and I would try and sell some bric-a-brac. Necessity is often the mother of invention, and so it proved in my case. This is how the next phase of my life began some thirty years ago—at our first venue, Silverwell Street in Bolton.

7
TOY FAIRS

We booked a table at a toy fair where David was successful in selling his model trains. I think we took around £300, which, at that time, was a lot of money. That night I went into the bathroom where David was in the bath, sucking the sponge, but with a smile on his face—yes, a smile.

'I really enjoyed today,' he said.

My God, he enjoyed himself. We discussed what we should do with the money. He gave me around £120 and told me to find a warehouse where I could buy model cars, while he advertised for more secondhand railways. This we did. However, being a born entrepreneur and a sucker for old, dusty items (it was in my blood), I arrived home with boxes of Triang tinplate tunnels, tinplate stations, old flying machine kits, *Man from Uncle* badges, *Lady from Uncle* guns, 007 models, you name it. I did not know the value or collectability of what I had bought, but with tinplate stations at 1/11d each—yes, one shilling and eleven old pence each (just under 10p), I knew I could not go wrong. I had bought a car full of dirty and dusty stock for about £100. The Triang tinplate stations were in boxes of six, and I had bought six boxes. Needless to say, David was expecting brand new models, and I had turned up with junk. He thought I had wasted the money and said he would not allow any of it in the house. He did not speak to me for hours.

David had already booked a table at a toy fair the following weekend in Buxton, so he reluctantly agreed that I could go with him to try and sell my secondhand acquisitions. To say the least I was deprived of sleep that night as, being utterly clueless about my boxes of 'junk', I imagined other dealers smiling at the pathetic display of collectibles I had to sell.

We arrived at the venue. David, being David, put all his items, boxes duly polished and displayed, in an orderly manner on the table. He told me to lay out my items on the remaining twelve inches or so he allowed me. I put out the *Man from Uncle* badges, just one card, then the *Lady from Uncle* guns, and the 007 plastic rafts, blue and green fluorescent pieces of plastic, which were placed at the bottom of a box with the top partly cut off. They were quite revolting really. The dealer on the stall opposite could see that I was a first-time dealer with an assortment of unusual models. He came over.

'How much are the badges?' he asked.

'A pound each.'

'How many have you got?'

'Just this one card.'

'I'll take it.'

Then he pointed at the guns. 'How much are these?'

'Three pounds each.'

'How many have you got?'

'Three,' I replied.

'I'll take all three.'

Then he looked at the rafts. I began to think some dealing was called for.

'Seven pounds each,' I told him.

'I'll take them all.'

By this time, other dealers could see that something out of the ordinary was occurring on David's table, nothing to do with his trains, but rather with my junk, my beautiful, dusty junk. Someone then tried to get items out of the box under the table, but I asked him politely to wait. The next item out of the box was a display card full of what looked like cheap and nasty Noddy rings and broaches.

Somebody asked, 'How much?'

'Ten pence each.'

'I'll take the full card,' said the dealer.

More dealers gathered around the table.

The doors to the venue had not even opened yet and I had sold all my stock—£360 in my pocket and a big smile on my face. I had left a lot more similar items at home, not thinking that my junk was other people's gold and I already couldn't wait to return with my bounty.

The following week I requested a day's leave from work. I telephoned the warehouse to see if I could spend some time there, and looked forward to buying another car full of dusty, dirty junk. I remember that day clearly. For the most part I was rummaging through the top shelf where all the non-saleable items had been put. I will try and describe some of these items.

There were glass slides, hand-painted with about six pictures on each slide, highly coloured, glossy postcards from the 1930s, 1:72 Matchbox models, car racing sets from the 1950s, similar to Scalextric. The best item I bought literally fell on my head from the top shelf. It was a green plastic ball with orange bits of plastic stuck on. The label said, "I am a Meccanoid from the Dr Who series."

'How many of these have you got?' I asked.

'Twenty-three,' the lady said.

'How much?'

'Five shillings eleven pence.'

She then asked if she could charge me thirty new pence each (equivalent to six shillings in old money). I took all twenty-three. I thought I could probably sell them for £1 each.

I went home with my dirty treasures and put them in the garage, out of sight and out of mind, and never said a word to David about what I had bought.

The day after my trip to the warehouse I received a phone call from someone in London.

'Are you the lady who sold the Dr Who rafts in Buxton? If I tell you how much I paid for them, could I come to Preston to see what else you have?'

He then asked if there was anything else of interest.

'A Meccanoid from the Dr Who series,' I said, as if I knew what I was talking about.

Imagine a sharp intake of breath.

'Yes,' he said. 'How many have you got?'

'Ten.'

'How much?'

'Twenty-five pounds each.'

'I'll take all ten.'

That was more than eighty times what I had paid for them. He made arrangements to come to Preston the following day and, within half an hour, had given me £500 for the ten Meccanoids and other goods of a similar nature.

As he was departing, he turned back and asked, 'You don't have any more of these Meccanoids, do you? Because if you are going to sell here, I am not going to get my price in London.'

When I said that I had another thirteen and definitely no more, he took all the stock. My mind then went into overdrive. I could not sleep that night and decided it would be better for me to take a week off work and buy more stock, the older the better.

David and I discussed opening a model railway shop to sell his railway stock. He found an empty, rundown shop in Preston near a viaduct. At least the rent was cheap. And so we became shopkeepers. For the time being I would keep my job with the Civil Service and help David on Saturdays in the shop, and on Sundays I would go to car boot sales in order to sell some of my ever increasing stock of collectibles.

Shopkeepers should be friendly people with an optimistic outlook in life, and always a pleasure to see. David, although basically a nice person, did not fit this criteria. He tried his best, but always looked on the black side. He never had enough money to pay the bills, so he smoked more and more, and complained more and more.

For my part, I tried selling modern, highly polished Corgi cars in new boxes. This was disastrous. My first attempt was to sell the Corgi Penny Post tram and boxed Minnie the Minx cars. David and I went to a Manchester toy fair, Bowlers, with stock we had purchased from a wholesaler. We duly laid out the new boxed Corgis on the table. I cannot remember the exact prices, but say the Minnie the Minx set was selling for £15, we put on £15. After we had set out the stall, I scouted the fair to find out what other dealers were selling. The dealer on the next table had the same item on at £14.50, then the man lower down was selling for £14. By the time I got back to our table in this vast hall, vendors were selling for a price lower than we had bought for. I have hated toy fairs and new stock ever since.

8

THE LAWSON STREET SHOP

One day David came home and said that two people had been in the shop, a father and son, who said they had spent quite a lot of money on model railways and were really pleased that David had opened the shop. They gave him an initial order for some model railway accessories: two right-hand points, two left-hand points, a crossing, and various other items. All very well, you might think. But these points had to be bought in full boxes, ten per box; so to sell two, you had to buy ten. The track, which came in small, medium and large sections, were in boxes of twenty-four or thirty-six. We had to offer a general selection of railway track in the shop, but it was going to cost ten times more than we could afford. This became the general rule of thumb for the next few years. We always had to spend more than we sold, which generated credit card bills by the dozen, as well as an ever increasing overdraft (that was when the banks were being good to us).

Every Sunday I would go to the car boot sale in Clitheroe at 4 a.m. I put my items on the trestle tables and I would do quite well, but the money raised would be quickly absorbed by David.

I am not a fool, never have been and never will be. Having worked for the Crown Prosecution Service and the Official Receiver, all outgoing monies were accounted for in my accounts, so that when it came to the parting and divorce, I could clearly show where my money had gone.

I was known as the train lady in Clitheroe and soon had regular buyers. As my knowledge of model railways was very limited, I generally priced the trains depending on their length, condition, and whether they were boxed or not. Some customers bought highly collectible kit-built items, and because they were generally short in length, I would sell them as I would other small engines at, say £10 each, whereas they were often worth over £70.

Three years after opening the shop in Preston, a bigger shop became vacant near Preston Police Station. The father and son that I mentioned earlier came to help David install shelving. They were both skilled joiners and by the end of the first week we were ready to open an upmarket model shop. By this time David had started selling model cars and other items which fell under the description 'models'. Mark, the younger joiner, told David that plastic kits, such as Airfix, were very popular and suggested he stock some in the shop. This was one of the best pieces of advice he ever received, as this side of the business grew. But the success came with a logistical problem. Because kits came in larger boxes, some very large, it soon became obvious that the shop was going to be too small.

Fortuitously for us there was a model shop in Preston that had suffered a fire. It had closed down, but the shop was still full of stock. The larger items had been sold in an auction, but all the ancillary items, such as paints, glues, track, grasses for railways, spare parts by the hundreds, were still in situ. The owner of the shop next door had acquired the premises but did not want the stock. I took myself off to have a word with him. I negotiated a figure of £7,500 for the stock, and went home to tell David. As we certainly didn't have £7,500 at that time, it meant we would have to borrow the money, and the only way we could do this was to take out a second charge on our home. 'Never,' was David's blunt response.

After I managed to borrow the money from the bank I hired a transit van to bring all the stock home. We had just decorated the spare room downstairs and installed new French windows, new carpet, and the room looked perfect. But not for long. The enormous amount of stock filled the room from floor to ceiling. I will not—and could not—describe David's reaction, so you will have to use your imagination. David refused to sell this stock, but I did. I still have spares which proved invaluable in later years.

Despite the excitement of the new business and all the potential for growth, David's depressive outlook on life was unbearable. I suggested to him that he was not making me happy, and I was certainly not making him happy, and never could. I asked if he wanted to 'call it a day'. He quickly agreed. To cut a long story short, he soon found another soulmate, decided he had had enough of the shop, and transferred the business to Wales. Six months later, he was bankrupt.

This is when I became a full-time model shop proprietor.

9
TRANSPORT MODELS

Mark (the joiner who had worked for David on Saturdays for a few years in the Preston shop) telephoned me to ask what was the current situation, as David had not mentioned his move to Wales. He was a good worker, so it was suggested that he should leave his present job, borrow some money from relatives, so that we could become partners. Being by now sixty-one, I had just retired from the Civil Service so I could work in the shop whenever necessary. We continued trading as Transport Models in the small shop for the next four years. As the business was slowly expanding and there was not enough room for the additional stock we carried, we moved to Oyston Mill where there was plenty of parking. Within a month, due to the added advantage of the car park, our turnover had doubled.

We then contacted our accountants and filed the necessary papers to become a limited company, not because we were worried about future debts, but to put the business on a firmer footing. We also helped other model shops to continue in business when their cash flow came under pressure. This was especially the case with a shop in Southport that we realised would not survive in its present form. We arranged a deal with the owner in which he would work for us, while we would take over his assets and liabilities to keep the business afloat. We revamped the shop, redecorated and filled it to capacity with stock.

At the end of our financial year we found that, although we had doubled the turnover in the new shop, our combined net profit was the same as the previous year. The manager now told us that he had been offered a job on the railways and was leaving. Mark and I discussed putting in another manager but decided against it. We closed the shop in Southport in the hope the customers would travel to our shop in Preston.

Everyone knows Mark as the quiet one. No one would describe him as a happy person, but he is always the life and soul of any private party, of which he has many. His knowledge of all aspects of the stock is brilliant. It is why we have been successful. He controls the incoming new products, knows the popularity of stock, and is highly respected by the directors of model manufacturers. I, on the other hand, still like secondhand models, buying collections, whether railway or diecast, and in some cases plastic kits.

When we first started Transport Models Limited we had never heard of eBay. I was introduced to this avenue of selling by a friend who sat me down at the computer to open an account with an ID and selling name. No matter what name we picked—modelspreston, prestonmodels, or anything with the name model in it—eBay would not allow it.

After an hour, my friend asked, 'What do you sell?'

'Kits.'

'You are a lady.'

'What about Kitlady.'

Hence our current trading name on eBay.

We sell a lot of the items that I find in collections on eBay, and have always had excellent backing from them. Although their commission is high, eBay must have saved thousands of small businesses from insolvency as they have been able to recoup money from the sale of old, unsold stock.

I have always bought new Corgi stock, but only had interest in TV-related items as these seemed to hold their value, whereas the general items were liable to drop in value only a week after purchase. Other dealers were offering such high discounts that in general the new stock was lower in value than the price we had paid for it. I have complained to Corgi so many times about differing discounts given to dealers, who in turn would always undercut everyone else. On one particular day I bought twenty-four large, modern trucks. In general I bought these for around £34, the selling price earmarked at £60. The same weekend they were being offered in a collectors' magazine for £25. I had a few hundred of these modern trucks, as well as all the other Corgi models on my shelves. I could not put a value on my existing stock because it had devalued so much. I called in the accountants who advised that at my year-end I had to put the lower value. It was pointless stating that they were worth the price I paid when they were being sold cheaper everywhere else.

We were not the only company dealt these blows. One by one our model shop neighbours went out of business—firstly

Lancaster, then Red Bank Road, Blackpool, Lytham St Annes, Darwen, Preston and Blackburn. These unfortunate shop owners had, by all accounts, borrowed money to buy their stock, which had devalued within a few weeks. The manufacturer was selling direct to the general public at a lower price than they sold to the shops, so it was cheaper for the shops to buy at the same price as the public. It was an untenable situation for a retailer.

The same irregularities were occurring all over England; consequently model shops have declined rapidly. This has eventually backfired on certain manufacturers as they do not have the same number of retail outlets that used to display their products to the public. The manufacturers are still managing to rely on internet sales, but where can people go to see, touch and try out their products on display?

10

JIM – MY THIRD

I had been working in the model railway shop for about two years when, one Sunday, being very bored with my own company, I saw an advertisement for a new dating agency in Preston. I filled in the appropriate details and sent off an application. Having second thoughts, when the person from the agency telephoned me to make arrangements for an interview, I very nicely said that I had changed my mind.

'Are you on your own now?' she asked.

'Yes,' I said.

'Well just come and have a talk to us, there is nothing to lose, is there?'

I went for the interview, paid my fees and I joined the agency.

Anyone who knew me would probably have asked, why? I was in a shop all day with men visiting aplenty. But these are model railway men. Nice people, very nice people, brilliant customers, but I did not want another model railway man filling my bedrooms with trains. He could look like a god, have a brilliant body, and have loads and loads of money, but no, I was not going down that road again.

The first introduction from the dating agency was to a man named Jim who wore a hearing aid. I met him in a pub halfway between Preston and Blackpool, where he lived. My first impression was that he was very pleasant, but he held no attraction for me. After half an hour he got hold of my hand—which was not a good move to a former convent girl. This was a bad sign and I went home a little disappointed. The girl at the agency told me not to expect much from the first date, but to go on a second with an open mind to see if there were better vibes. For the second date Jim turned up in a suit and tie, very different from the previous occasion and very, very smart. I still had no physical attraction for him, but said I would go out with him again some time in the future, not just yet. These occasional dates continued on and off, going nowhere romantic, but staying friends.

The fees I paid to the dating agency allowed me to have introductions to six men, so I still had to see another five. And what a bunch they were! One had to use an inhaler after walking ten yards and appeared to be on his last legs; one had a single tooth at the front; another had bad breath, which I could smell from the other side of the table. He thought he had met his future wife, but I told him differently. The fourth was an accountant who rang most nights, often filling my answerphone with dull information. That went nowhere. The agency suggested they introduce me to a postman, but when I said one already came to my door every morning free of charge, I think they gave up on me. They did tell me they had an abundance of women but no decent men. Now you tell me!

I suppose I still had Jim to fall back on, who I carried on meeting on odd occasions for the next two years. Once I got to know him better I could see he was a nice person with a good sense of humour. He grew on me. He must have felt the same because we both sold our respective houses and began living together. Unfortunately I did not have a lot of money from the sale of my home because I had borrowed against it to fund my business purchases. Conversely, he had quite a lot of equity when he sold his home, which enabled us to buy a house. The solicitors were kept informed about the financial arrangements, so that Jim's family would be entitled to the estate should anything happen to him.

In many ways Jim was a gentleman—he did what I want men to do, that is, open the garage doors to let me out in the morning, make sure the car windows are not steamed up, and, if frozen, to unfreeze the car so it is warm for me to travel to work. He put the bins out every Monday, he was a brilliant gardener—our lawns were immaculate and straight—the toilet roll holders were never without a toilet roll, and any electrical faults were sorted with help from his son. On returning home each evening after work, he would have my usual evening drink ready in an ice-cold glass with a slice of lemon. We would then relax and discuss the day's activities. I usually made the meals. That is how it was, and that was how I liked it.

He could never muster any interest in my work, my shop, or my habitual credit card borrowings for the next influx of secondhand goods. After twenty years buying and selling model railways, you would think I'd know these models by their technical names. But I don't. I know what the Flying Scotsman looks like, and the Mallard, but why some Mallards are blue and others green is beyond me. Anyway, I have staff with the relevant professional skills to share with our customers. As long as I can sell everything I buy at a good profit, I am happy.

Jim may not have been interested in my work, but he liked money. He picked up pennies to save and put small change away. When there was enough to hand, he would bank it. He never understood why I would not put my money in ISAs, and yet would borrow a few thousand pounds to buy stock. When he did come to the shop, I would show him the bulging shelves, but he always said that money is only money when the item is sold, which is true, but businesses do not work that way. He was very popular and made me laugh, something the first two husbands certainly didn't.

We had never married, but six years after meeting Jim was diagnosed with cancer, and we made it formal. Before I met Jim he was an engineer. On retiring, as he loved gardening, he got a job as a gardener at the convent in Lytham St Annes. Jim liked ladies. One of his favourite phrases was, 'My ambition is to fill the roll of Lady Chatterley's lover'—but this was off limits in the convent.

He died in 2014.

11

THE BOOK AND MY CUSTOMERS

I had always planned to write this book when I retired. However, I have had sleepless nights with stories going around and around in my head, remembering times both good and bad (some very, very bad), and decided now was the time to share them. When the words are flowing, the little boxes with hidden memories open up. And even now, although I think I have written it all down, I will remember some other details and I go back to fill in the gaps. Most of these additional memories are from my early days, so not really important to my model railway fans, but maybe to the people who knew me at school. Probably a lot of them are dead, but I am not, so will continue planning for the future.

I shall now continue my story, which is mainly regarding Transport Models. I will try and give some encouragement to entrepreneurs who are generally of the opinion that opening a model shop is a good idea. Yes, it is a very good idea, as long as your pockets are wide and full, the bank manager is sympathetic (if there are any left), and the customers support you, and do not rely on internet sales all the time. It takes an enormous amount of effort every day to remain successful. By the way, success is not all down to one person's effort in a model shop, there is also the input from your staff (if you can afford to employ any), and luck.

When my second husband departed for the Welsh hills to set up his own model shop, my new business partner Mark and I were lucky. The Lawson Street shop had a fantastic reputation and was supported by customers who are still loyal to this day. This was at a time when Corgi produced some very good models. The order book was excellent and a lot of the stock which came into the shop went out on the day it arrived, as eager customers waited for the parcels to arrive on a Thursday. The bestsellers were the TV-related items—James Bond, Noddy, Inspector Morse's Jaguar, and others, which are still sought after today.

One day one of my customers came into the shop with his dog. As I was talking to him a couple came into the shop who I recognised as potential shoplifters from previous visits when stock had disappeared. I asked the customer to keep an eye on them. He sat on a chair, dog at his side, with a determined look on his face.

'They will take nothing while I am here,' he said.

The man stayed at the bottom of the shop and the woman came to the area where my customer was sitting. On the paint rack close by was a statue of a horse with a Star Trek figure. The lady then said to her husband, 'I have finished here,' and they both left the shop. My customer commented on the fact that you had to watch these people. I then realised that the statue had disappeared. My customer wonders to this day how she managed to take it without us noticing.

At this time we moved to larger premises in Oyston Mill.

Some readers may be interested to find out about model railways. But I am not going to explain the various categories and scales, etc. I would rather spend more time describing my customers and what inspires them to—I can't say play—but involve themselves with this particular hobby, and collecting in general.

Firstly, we have the *Track-putter-downer*. This is a man who loves trying to build the ultimate railway track. He wants to make the perfect layout, generally fails, buys more track and starts again, and again, and again.

Secondly we have *The purist*, who knows exactly which train ran where, in what shade of green, blue or black, and the correct coaches that accompanied the locomotive. He will not tolerate inaccuracies.

Next, we have the person who buys both secondhand and new trains, irrespective of whether they ran together or not. He is a prolific buyer, and generally a good customer. After about two years he will lose attraction for the hobby and will bring it all back to resell to us.

Then we have my favourites. These are families that will build a layout engine by engine. They will buy a blue train one day, a green one the next and, if you could get pink and blue coaches, would buy them too so as to make the layout more attractive. They will even put American trains on a British layout because they like the look of them (which would appal the purist). They generally enjoy the hobby immensely.

One of my friendly customers is a man called Brian. Now Brian hails from my part of England, which is Blackburn, and, whether or not I am biased, I like Blackburn people. They are generally the salt of the earth, speak with a northern accent, and call a spade a spade. Brian is certainly one of these. He will call into the shop at regular intervals, and always makes sure I know he is in the shop. He is six feet tall and has a wide beaming smile, but is toothless, and always confirms that he is the same age as me. He is not really; he is three months older. The age shows; hopefully more in him than myself. Have you seen a six-foot man cry? Well, one day Brian cried. He came into the shop, carrier bags in both hands and asked to see me. He said that he had to sell his model railway. I asked him not to cry, but he said he was waiting for eye drops from the doctors. Apparently his son had left his wife and wanted to move back home, and Brian's wife, Vera, dictated that 'the railway had to go'. Brian did as he was told, and brought his railway for me to buy. He was a pure model railway fan. These men, some of whom have even driven steam trains in the past, have lived for the time when their children have left home and there is a spare bedroom. However, children have a habit of returning back to mum and dad. I am glad to write that Brian now has his hobby room back and has happily bought a new layout.

A person who I will always remember was called Ian who was not into model railways, but collected buses. He told me one day that he had cancer and had been given about three months to live. He was an avid collector of local buses, but also had a keen interest in London buses. As I habitually bought collections, I would keep the London buses to one side so that Ian could check whether or not he already had them in his collection. He always placed an order for newly manufactured local buses, especially Ribble. Meanwhile Ian seemed to be cheating death. He kept being given a few months extension of his prognosis, until one customer told me that he had seen Ian in the hospice. Not good news. Two days later the shop door opened and in came Ian, supported on one side by his wife and on the other by his wife's brother. Ian's face broke into a smile when he saw the latest issue of stock, which his wife paid for. He returned to the hospice where he died two days later. This is a true collector. They will collect until they drop.

After Ian died, his wife approached me regarding all the buses she had acquired—and did not want.

'What do I do, Liz? All the buses are in cabinets all over the house and the boxes are in the attic. I don't know which bus goes into which box.'

I told her to throw the boxes away, bring all the buses to me and I would sell them unboxed. It would have cost me more in manpower to try and put all the buses back, than their worth. She brought them in three stages, as there were over 1,000. Over the years I have sold them all.

Another nice event happened when two elderly ladies came into the shop. One asked me if I bought model cars. She explained that she had contacted a well-known auction house and they had informed her that the cars were of no real value, and recommended she took them to a model shop. She placed six cars on the counter: Models of Yesteryear. These models were made in their thousands, and now and again one will have been produced with either a variation of colour, or wheel, which makes it collectible. I told her this and she looked crestfallen. It is difficult to assess why people want to sell. It could be that a small amount of extra money would help to pay an outstanding bill. I never truly know. The woman said that she had quite a lot of models at home in Leyland, which was in the opposite direction to my usual drive home to Blackpool. Plus, at that time, my husband was very ill. I told her I would come to her house after work but I could not stay long.

When I arrived the two ladies were sitting on the settee with two boxes between them, and a young boy who was presumably her grandson. I took one of the boxes and laid the cars on the floor in order—Matchbox of Yesteryear, some Solido, then one or two Dinkies. Meanwhile the grandson went upstairs and brought another box and placed it on the settee. Time was passing and I was worried about leaving my husband for so long. I phoned home and told Jim I would be another hour. By this time the floor was filled with boxed cars, some very good, some mediocre and, of course, the unsaleable ones.

The lady then apologised profusely for asking me to call when the cars were not worth very much. On the contrary, I told her, I was already up to over a thousand pounds.

'Oh my God,' she said, 'did you say over £1000?'

There were still more boxes to unearth on the settee. Eventually I reached the last box, which was filled with lead animals, each one wrapped in newspaper. By this time I really had to leave.

'Can I do a deal with you?' I said. 'I haven't time to unwrap all these. I've got the total up to £1,400 so far. Can I make it £1,500 including whatever's in this last box?'

I don't think her face had resumed its normal colour after I had told her the first time how much her collection was worth, but to see her face and the reaction was absolutely marvellous. I don't think she had ever seen £1,500 in cash before.

Generally wives tolerate, to some extent, their husband's hobby. This was particularly true with one couple. Every time they came into the shop, swear words hung in the air and it was a battle zone. The wife would say no, and the husband insisted yes.

'If I want it, I'm having it!'

This happened each time they entered the shop. However, one day the wife came into the shop with her husband in a wheelchair linked up to an oxygen bottle.

'What is wrong?' I asked.

'Lung cancer,' he said.

This time he was quiet and his wife obeyed his commands.

Two months later his wife and daughter came into the shop first thing in the morning.

'Liz,' she said, 'can we empty the two cars at the door? They are both full.'

The staff then brought in a stack of boxes, and I told her that I would have to ring her with a price.

'Don't ring tomorrow,' she said, 'it is the funeral.'

After everything was sorted, or so I thought, she asked if she could bring in all his books.

She was quite an attractive woman, so I said to her, 'What if you met someone else and they said they liked model railways, what would you do?'

'Run a mile,' she replied. (This is a polite version of what she actually said.)

'Never, never again,' were her final words.

I haven't seen her since.

One customer who worries me is called Reg. He has been buying small trucks and buses—thousands of them!—from Transport Models for years, and from me personally since before I was a shopkeeper. He is the same age as me, but for the past forty years has suffered with heart problems. He has one son who has no interest whatsoever in models, so when Reg no longer has any interest in models, or is unable to handle his hobby, where is his collection going? I know he cuts up the models and glues wagons together, repaints and generally takes the collectability out of them, but I keep reminding his son about his potential inheritance. He says nothing, and just smirks.

At times a model shop is similar to a pawnbroker's; except, we buy back the same items, sometimes from different people, day after day. I am sure some of the Hornby wagons have run around most of the railway layouts in my area, as the same wagons come back day after day and go back into the secondhand corner to be sold time and time again. Hornby must have produced thousands of any one particular truck year in, year out, and I presume they will be reproduced in later years, but at a price far exceeding my, as new, preowned ones.

Years ago model railways, kits, buses and similar toys were not collected, but actually played with. As the majority of trains are now in the region of £100 and over, they are not designed for children, but for the older generation or collectors. When Christmas comes you can see parents in the shop discussing setting up a model railway layout for their child or grandchild. When I ask the age of the boy and they say four years old, I advise them to wait until they are older, or give them any old train and truck and let the child play. Give them cardboard, scissors and clay and ask them to make hills, roads, etc. No, the dad wants to play beforehand and build a state of the art layout for his—older than he appears—child. When the little boy comes down on Christmas morning, the proud parent unveils the masterpiece, sets the train and trucks rolling around, and the enthusiastic, or not so enthusiastic, child disappears to play with the empty boxes. The layout is left undisturbed and is then packed away. I have had this discussion with so many parents. Please let your child play, let him/her use their imagination. Does it matter if the cows are massive and the chickens as large as dinosaurs? The trains are generally pushed, and the wagons filled with anything that is loose, including soil, coal, and flour if it gets in the vicinity of tiny fingers. Also, a model like the Flying Scotsman, although a sought after loco by the fathers, are too big for tiny hands and hard to put on the track. Dads like to think their offspring are brighter than the ones next door, but this is generally not the case.

When I first opened the shop there were at least five model shops in Preston. Now we appear to be the only one left displaying model railways in the various liveries. Most of these are too expensive for children, but we need to attract young people so that the hobby continues. The manufacturers appear to be blind to some extent, and instead of encouraging shops to display stock, with increased discounts for larger purchases, they are reducing what is a very limited discount band. The general public will not understand why a man selling chips and fish can obtain specialised products direct from the wholesalers at the same price we pay. Unless the manufacturers realise that for a shop to employ staff with technical knowledge, and pay large overheads for shop premises to attract genuine buyers, the hobby will have no foundation to keep going. Online retailers can and will sell at a discount, but these people do not display products, nor offer technical advice. Could we make our business more profitable by only selling online? Some good manufacturers will only supply retailers with shop premises that open five days a week, and I certainly admire their ethics, but I am sure they will have to alter their sales techniques and open up their sales areas to include the online sellers.

When I leave the shop it is going to be difficult to find someone with the knowledge of the old collectible toy stock and I cannot download my knowledge on to a memory stick. Maybe one day this will be attempted, but certainly not in my time.

There is one saving grace, however, and that is eBay. It is rare not to find a product on this platform. eBay can give a general guide of an item's value, but there are lots of no-no's to this. To quote an example, it is possible to buy on eBay an apparently mint Corgi truck, in a mint box, for £60. But if the seller has been a smoker, the smell adheres to the truck, and no amount of perfume can get rid of it, especially to someone who hates the smell of cigarette smoke.

This reminds me of a customer I once had. Another Ian. He collected model trucks, and spent a lot of money with me. Whenever he called into the shop I would always make him a cup of coffee and he would bring me up to date with the news from his family. Ian's wife had died a few years before, so he lived on his own. The shared cup of coffee and his purchases were something for him to look forward to. However, one day, not long after Ian had been in the shop, two customers asked to see someone regarding buying some trucks. They had been clearing out the belongings of their father who was recently deceased and had found one of our receipts in a box. They enquired whether or not we would buy them back. I asked them who their father was, and they told me his name. It was Ian. Being utterly devastated I could not speak, turned and went back to my office. I told the staff to take a phone number and I would ring them back. Even now, typing this narrative, I am getting a lump in my throat, as he was a genuine friend and nice person. I was very worried about the stock Ian had bought from me as he was a very heavy smoker, mostly cigars. However, he had bought a lot of plastic boxes with lids and his stock was, for the most part, cigar smell-free.

I have lost so many customers who became friends over the years. I realise that no matter how you love your model railways, buses, kits or cars, these are only items of a specific value and cannot return your love. They are generally sold on to the next person, and the next, and the next until they disintegrate or are found in an attic many years hence.

Sound knowledge of secondhand stock is paramount in my job. I had to go to Widnes one Tuesday after a woman telephoned to say that her father had died. She had come all the way from Canada to sort out the house with her brother, but was returning home on the Friday. The woman had only two hours free, so I took one of my staff and turned up at the terraced house. The downstairs front room, middle room and hallway were filled to the brim with boxes, and the walls were covered with display cabinets crammed with locos. There was no room to test or see the stock properly. I went from cabinet to cabinet, calling out a price as I went, then I rifled through all the boxes, under the bed, on top of the bed, and the same upstairs. After two hours, her time limit, I offered a price of £14,500. 'I would have liked more,' she said. I explained that no way could I improve as I did not know whether all the locos worked, and whether the labelling on the boxes was accurate. I suggested she try another dealer to compare prices. She then asked how I would pay her and said that she wanted the money in her bank by the following day as the house had to be emptied completely before she returned home on the Friday morning. The deal was done. I arranged with the bank to transfer the money, hired a transit van and emptied the house.

This visit was a good example of why I love my job. Do I envy the dentist who looks into the mouths of his patients? Certainly not. He may have a big bank balance, a lot bigger than mine, but I have surprises every day, opening all the boxes which are brought into me containing people's collections.

12

RETIREMENT

I planned to retire at the end of June 2018, but again, planning and actually carrying out this transition to a more relaxed way of life has not happened. In preparation for my retirement I bought stacks of art canvasses, acrylic paint of every colour and brushes by the dozen. I painted some abstract art—very abstract!—that looks colourful hanging on my walls. Anyone who shows an interest, even though it may be a purely encouraging gesture, usually goes home with one or two tucked under their arms. It is doubtful whether any of these paintings will hang in an art gallery, but I like them.

I have to mention here two of my customers, Brian and Linda. They come from Chorley, speak with a broad Lancashire dialect where a head is an 'ed'. They are definitely two of my favourite customers—down to earth, loyal and love coming to the shop. Linda always makes sure Brian goes home with a bag of goodies.

One of my first paintings was quite good. It was bright yellow and, if you had a good imagination, you could see mountains in the distance, topped with snow, and with a little greenery here and there. To show my appreciation of their custom, I gave the painting to Brian and Linda. It is in their dark hallway, but it is so bright, it brings light to a shady corridor.

Someone has suggested that I should take up golf. Little do they know that I did try it many years ago, in my early twenties. I went for golf lessons over the winter months, practising in a hut with a string net hanging halfway across the room. The professional who took the lessons said that I had a brilliant swing, despite the fact that I never seemed to hit the ball straight. It either went to the right or the left. It was decided that I needed shorter golf clubs, but finances would not stretch to new clubs, so I had some of my husband's cut down—but still the balls went left or right, never straight.

Somehow I managed to play three rounds of golf before I was given the mandatory lady beginners' handicap of thirty-six. My first competition was the following week—Captain's Day, one of the biggest club competitions of the year. Who was drawn out of the hat to play with the captain? Me.

The captain walked out of the clubhouse to a resounding applause from all his faithful club members as he approached the first tee. Nervously I followed. He duly placed the ball on the tee and lined up the customary practice swing. Again, applause from the onlookers. He addressed the ball, swung his club, and completely missed his shot, the ball rolling off the tee with the draught from his swing. As he had technically played a shot, it was then my turn. In front of the gathering golfers, I swung, hit the ball, and sent it skywards before it dropped a few feet away and rolled down the side of the first tee. At least it had gone further than the captain's effort.

Then it started to rain, and it went downhill from there. Being a beginner, I did not have the correct headgear and walked around the whole course with a knitted woollen hat, which soaked up the rain and continually unravelled about my face. It was a wet, uncomfortable, seemingly endless afternoon. I don't think the poor man will ever forget what could (and should) have been the most memorable day of his golfing year as captain.

Not to be beaten, a few days afterwards I decided to try again. I lived in a place called Wilpshire, opposite the entrance to the golf course. I went to the first tee with ten balls, put down the first, then the second, and hit them one by one. I sent each ball either to the left into the plots or to the right into a small wooded area. I decided to take the last three balls to another hole, a par four. A road cut this fairway into two sections, which would normally take me three attempts to cross. On this occasion there were two young boys waiting to tee off. The first one put his ball down and, after a wiggle or two of the hips and a practice swing, he addressed the ball and, pulling his right arm down, hit the ball straight down the middle and over the road. The second boy did the same, again with the definite wiggle, and straight down the middle it went.

As soon as they were out of range, I copied what I had seen. I put the ball on the tee, a wiggle of the hips, a practice swing, and then whacked the ball. There was a nice subdued click and it soared off into the distance. At that time I had a stigma in one eye, so had difficulty in assessing where the ball had actually gone. I walked after it and looked in the usual places, then I heard the boys shout, 'Hey missus, your ball is over here.' It had landed over the road, further than I'd ever hit the ball before.

Highly delighted, I lined up my second stroke, again with the same nonchalant movement of the hips, arm down to my side, and heard the nice 'click'. The boys again told me where my ball had gone, this time landing just before the green. I chipped it on to the green—an incredible three strokes to the green! I was on course to score par at a par four hole! However, I could not putt, never have been able to, and used up another six strokes before the unco-operative ball finally went down the hole.

I went home and told my husband that I had found the secret to playing good golf, but later that week found out I was pregnant and never went on the course again.

13

OYSTON MILL AND MORE CUSTOMERS

I honestly do not know if this business will continue. Oyston Mill, our current premises, is owned by the Oyston family who have their own ideas about the building. We have been trading day to day for four years not knowing whether the mill is going to be used for student accommodation, auctioned off, or pulled down. My business partner is anxious to continue, either here or in alternative premises. The relationship between landlord—Denwis Limited (Mr Oyston's company)—and tenant—Transport Models—is getting worse every day. Although I have requested information about whether or not we can still run our business from Oyston Mill, this is not forthcoming. I have decided, therefore, in the interests of all concerned, to write a diary of events, intertwined with stories of the day to day happenings at the model shop.

August 4 2018
We were promised that a letter would be sent to all tenants on Wednesday, but it is now Saturday and nothing has been

received, so I have sent another email this morning asking for information.

Transport Models has a monthly licence with our landlords, which means they are only obliged to give us one month's notice to leave Oyston Mill. As we have been here for seventeen years, we have accumulated stock, display cupboards, computers, etc., which would take months to sell. Fearing the worst and with a heavy heart we therefore commenced a moving sale on Tuesday.

Six days before my eighty-third birthday, how can I plan a move to other premises with all the upheaval and work this will entail? I know there are four men on staff, but I could not face all the challenges such trauma will bring.

I am writing this diary to let budding entrepreneurs realise that, no matter how hard you try, and no matter how successful you are, you cannot foresee all the difficulties ahead. Some things are out of your control. We are now well established, financially secure, and should be reaping the rewards from all our hard work. Not to be.

Perhaps there is someone out there at this moment who would love to buy the mill, play with model railways, and convert the other units into one of the biggest hobby centres in England. That would be a lifesaver. I could have done this, and would still enjoy the challenge. Just imagine, Oyston Mill with a model centre, remote control unit, doll's house emporium, card and craft unit, knitting and embroidery section and a toy shop. The whole family could be catered for—children, wives, husbands and all the doting relatives.

Our stock sale so far has been very successful, but customers are requesting information about our future. Mark and I would also like to know the answer to this!

Wednesday, August 8 2018

No news. The sale is progressing well, but every one of our customers (and there are a lot) are asking questions about where we are moving to and when. We have to try to explain to all and sundry why we have to leave, but of course we are in the position of not knowing the answer ourselves.

I am going to email the accountants this afternoon to see if I can get some co-operation from them. Not only do our customers deserve some concrete news, our company insurance is due for renewal this month. As the annual premium is in the region of £2,000, we do not want to renew if we have to leave next month. But we have to have insurance.

One saving grace is that our finances are good. We have no worries at all in this direction, so we can keep smiling for the time being. As a matter of fact, if we keep selling and only buy absolute necessities, we will have more money in the bank than is usual at this time of year.

August 10 2018 – my 83rd birthday

I have tried to put down in this book events which have occurred in my life which would make for interesting reading, perhaps some less so, but the following happened to me as a young woman and it was quite terrifying. This was when I ventured into the psychic world.

I would have been about twenty-eight, living in the flat above my business premises in Preston New Road, Blackburn, and was having a pleasant weekend with my children. My husband, Ken, had gone to the Isle of Man for a short golfing holiday with friends, as he did quite regularly.

My younger daughter and son had gone to bed and I was in the lounge with my older daughter. There was a programme on television relating to mental telepathy and a presenter explained how you could communicate with another living person with whom you have a connection, say a sister or brother or someone very close. The programme was followed by the Last Night at the Proms. Having no interest, I said to my daughter that I would go and have a bath.

In my day to day business activities I had to visit some solicitors' offices to collect and distribute finished work, but this was only on a weekday, never at weekends. To be quite truthful, as my marriage at that time was not good, I had a schoolgirl crush on one of the solicitors with whom I came into contact. I would never have an illicit affair, as this was definitely not tolerated in the Catholic religion. However, as long as it was only a crush with no involvement, I was on safe ground. The solicitor lived with his mother, having just left his wife. I did not know his address, but knew that the house was situated on a road not far from my offices. I only called him by his surname and our paths never crossed other than through work.

That Saturday night, I ran the water for the bath, got in and relaxed. I thought of this solicitor, imagining him sitting in an upright armchair in an old-fashioned room. I focused my mind on him and willed him to walk to the telephone and dial my number. I mentally placed his finger into the dial. Astonishingly, at that moment my daughter knocked on the bathroom door and said the solicitor was on the phone asking for me. On a Saturday night? My legs were paralysed, I could not move, my heart was thudding.

I went to the telephone, voice shaking. He was calling about a mutual builder client who was golfing with my husband. The solicitor wanted a copy of the builder's letterhead so he could put a bid in to Blackburn Town Hall by 9 a.m. Monday morning. He arranged to visit that evening. I went to the door with my daughter next to me, the notepaper in my hands ready.

He said, 'Are you all right? You look pale.'

I answered in the affirmative, and gave him the piece of paper. Maybe he had other ideas and in truth the attraction was mutual. But I shall never know. He died some years ago.

My mother always said that she was psychic and she could feel if there was impending doom, but we always just smiled and nodded our heads in agreement. But perhaps she really did have powers, and maybe I have inherited some of her abilities.

Now that I am 83, what have I to look forward to? A fourth husband? I don't think so. Botox? I already have too many wrinkles. Plastic surgery? But that requires full body treatment. I am lucky to be as I am, so I'm just trying to stay happy.

I had a wonderful birthday. The family stayed with me for four days and I was at a loss after they left. Just for the one day

I felt as though I would like the 'problems' of having another husband, or even adopting a hyperactive two-year-old, but these feelings only lasted that one day. I am now back at work and my home is again spotless with the uninhabited look.

August 15 2018

Still no news. However, in the interim, I will write about one of my customers.

I told him that I would put in print his purchase history, but all he did was laugh. I gave him a copy of my first book and promised that he would be written about in later chapters.

Mr No-name started coming to the shop about four years ago. He absolutely loves locomotives, does nothing with them after purchase and keeps them in the carrier bags he takes them home in. He buys and buys and buys, which is very good, apart from the fact that he returns them some nine months later for me to buy back. He always apologises profusely for having to do this, but his finances deem this necessary. The first time he brought them back I gave him slightly less than the purchase price. Two or three months later he started buying again. After about six months of continuous buying, he again brought all his carrier bags full of locos and rolling stock to sell due to lack of finances.

I explained to him that, as much as I tried to refund at good prices, he was losing money on every return visit. Lightheartedly I warned him that he would be banned from the shop if he returned all his purchases again. His reply was that he loved trains and he would never return his purchases. I told the staff that Mr No-name could buy again, but he had to limit his purchases to a stipulated amount per month. He continued buying and his limit was soon exceeded but promised he was definitely going to keep his present acquisitions. Again he returned everything and explained the reasons. He is now banned from buying. He can come into the shop and look at the models, but look only. I wonder how long this will last. I am sure he will be on a buying spree again. He can't resist.

My friend, Arthur

Some thirty years ago, before I was a shopkeeper and only selling collectibles at Clitheroe car boot sale every Sunday, I heard from one of my customers that there was a man called Arthur in Blackburn who had a warehouse filled with boxes of old stock. My sister had a stall at that time on Blackburn Market, where Arthur had a stall selling toys. I found out where he was and made myself known to him. He looked just like my dad, another Arthur, so I took an instant liking to him. I told him I had heard about his old stock and asked if it would be possible for me to have a look around. He said quite adamantly 'No', and explained that he had only once let a dealer in, and a lot of stock had gone 'missing'.

I talked to Arthur and his wife for some time, telling him that my parents used to have a stall on the market, who he knew very well. Eventually he relented.

'Since I knew your parents and had known them for years, I will let you go in.'

He said that I could go with his wife, who at the time was in cancer remission. We made arrangements to go to the 'warehouse' which was, in fact, a Victorian terraced house. When his wife opened the front door there was a strong musty smell and all I could see were boxes and boxes and boxes. I could not get into the house unless I lifted a box and put it behind me. Thus I moved slowly throughout the house box by box.

Although by this time I knew a little about model railways, Corgi and other diecast models, the stock Arthur had accumulated was more to be described as boxed games, plastic and stuffed toys, dolls and accessories. Every time we opened a box it either contained mouldy and mildewed items, Airfix kits still in their plastic inner containers, but the outer box disintegrating due to damp, and lots of stock which should have been thrown on a skip. However, I did find some items that I liked (even though I knew little about them or their value), such as Barbie and Sindy models, and doll's clothes on cards.

That Sunday I took some of the items with me to Clitheroe, where the usual collectors sought me out to see what I had brought. One of these collectors was particularly knowledgeable, and he told me that some of the items that I was trying to sell for 50p were worth quite a lot more and that I should ask £10, as these were sought after in the doll trade.

What I am trying to explain here is that I have learned a lot from genuine people about what to buy and what to sell. I have visited lots of dirty, old-fashioned toy shops, warehouses, people's houses, and washed more toys to make them fit for sale than I have household clothes.

Shortly after I visited Arthur's warehouse, his wife became very ill and died. He found trade on his market stall to be very slow and, as he also had a stall on Fleetwood Market, he was unable to buy new stock through lack of ready cash.

By this time I had begun trading in the Lawson Street shop with Mark where we had plenty of new stock, especially Corgi. I made arrangements with Arthur that I would supply him with the new items of Corgi he needed for his regular customers, and I would take some of his old stock. He readily agreed. I would meet him on a pub car park in Blackburn to do a deal once a month and then go inside to have a meal. He thoroughly enjoyed this.

Unfortunately, a few months later Arthur was walking his rather large, old dog, which pulled him to the ground. Arthur was hurt quite badly, and had to go into hospital. Not long after, he died.

His relatives inherited all his belongings, house, warehouse and stock, but they did not contact me, so they must have had their own way of selling everything.

I really missed Arthur, but I am sure he, like me, enjoyed the swapping of stock and the nights out.

Tuesday, August 28 2018

This was a bad day for us at Transport Models, and for the other Oyston Mill unit holders. We received notification from the electricity suppliers to the mill that our power was going to be disconnected due to non-payment of the account by the landlord. In fact, tenants have not been able to pay their electricity bills to the landlords due to an ongoing dispute relating to Blackpool Football Club, which has frozen Mr Oyston's bank accounts. The tenants have money set aside, so there is a substantial amount due, which would be paid immediately the landlord's account is unfrozen.

Meanwhile we live in fear that the electricity could be disconnected at any moment. If the account is not paid today, we will have to start packing all the stock ready for a move to alternative premises next week. There are thousands of items which have to be boxed and catalogued. Once the electricity is turned off, the mill will have no lights or alarm systems, and therefore no entry will be permitted to anyone due to health and safety concerns.

Do I need this upset at my time of life? Certainly not. What can I do now to rectify the situation? That is today's ultimate question. A few weeks in the sun, near a white sandy beach, together with beach bars, would be one answer, but this is not an avenue open to me at the moment.

Three people with items for sale have telephoned me this morning asking if they could bring in their stock. I asked them to wait until I get firm news about our tenancy. Until then I will not be able to buy any extra stock. This is the most enjoyable part of my work, but as they say, all good things come to an end.

Wednesday, August 29 2018

The landlords have emailed to let the tenants know that all is well and the utility bills have been paid. We're saved! What we have to consider now is, do we want to continue at the mill knowing that we are going to have to face a big upheaval in the near future or stay here and hope for the best?

When I look back, a lot of the good, old-fashioned companies have recently gone out of business, such as Woolworths, British Home Stores, Toys R Us, which have left memories behind that will fade as the years go by. Do we close, and add to those memories? Luckily both partners, Mark and myself, have no financial worries as we have enough stock that should fund us through the next few years. What will not be so nice is saying goodbye to all our friends and loyal customers. I imagine it will be worse than going to a funeral.

This morning I have instructed the staff to bring down to the shop all the duplicate stock that is kept in the upstairs rooms. Even though we have had a sale for a few weeks, there are no empty shelves. We have decided to refrain from buying any more replacement stock, unless absolutely necessary, for the next two weeks at least.

Friday, August 31 2018

My good intentions, or not so good, regarding buying more stock has been voided. In other words, I bought another 100 locomotives today from one of my good customers, and also some oo gauge model railways from another 'used to be' customer, as he has had to give up his hobby due to ill health.

THE CHRONICLES OF A MARKET TRADER'S DAUGHTER FROM BLACKBURN

Saturday, September 1 2018

It is now 10.15 a.m. and I have already purchased another thirty locomotives. I can't stop myself. I wrote earlier that I would be selling all and retiring, but these plans are fading quickly. Another person has just telephoned to say he is on his way to see me with a large collection of cars. I am so lucky in one respect because I do not have to advertise for good pre-owned stock, but one day I am going to have to stop buying. Mark and I have always given a fair price for secondhand stock, even though we know customers rarely expect to sell for big money. We always work on the basis of two thirds to the customer and one third profit for us. It is nice to see the surprise they get when we quote a decent price.

Last week, Eric, a longstanding customer, brought all his railway in to sell. He was losing his sight and had fallen on hard times. After I had inspected all his stock, I asked him to write down on a piece of paper how much he wanted, but not to show it to me. I wrote down how much I was going to give him. He had written £750; I had written £1,250. He filled up with tears and thankfully shook my hand, saying that he could now clear all his debt and have a little left over. I gave him the cash and his wife put her arms around him and took him out of the shop. I think this is why we are so successful. I hope this little story will give hope to some men who have lost their wife and only have their model railways to keep them company.

A few years ago we started opening the shop on Sundays. The staff would be here for 9 a.m. but we didn't open the doors until ten o'clock. One winter's Sunday, raining hard, cold, dismal, I found a man on the doorstep waiting for the shop to open. I opened the main doors and told him to come into the shop, but I had to do quite a lot to make the shop ready for customers, so he had to amuse himself in the meantime. I asked him why he was out so early. At that point he burst into tears and told me that his wife had died and he did not know how to pass the time as he missed her so much. I made him a cup of coffee and told him about my husband who had lost his first wife, then met me, and his life was now happy again. I told him that there were a lot of ladies looking for male company.

A few months passed by and the man, escorted by two very attractive ladies, one on each arm, approached me at the counter. He reminded me of his previous visit on that cold Sunday morning, thanked me profusely, and told me that he was going to live down south with his soon-to-be wife (on one arm) and her sister (on the other). I have never seen him since, but I am sure he is now happy again.

Saturday, September 8 2018
Some tenants moved out today. The question is, do we stay until the bitter end or do we jump ship? The tenants who have left appear to be the ones who had rented rooms on the first floor. They did not want to be stranded with their heavy machinery upstairs in case the electricity was cut off. They had to use the lifts, but these would have been inoperable if there was no power.

On Sunday I looked around the Lytham, Blackpool and Ansdell areas to see if I could find any suitable accommodation, but most of the available units were far too large for us and very, very expensive.

Friday, September 14 2018
Apparently there have been newspaper reports in which I am alleged to have said that I would be more or less glad to leave. This is far from the truth, as I have found the premises spacious, especially for our disabled customers as it has easy access for wheelchairs and room enough between rows of display shelves for them to manoeuvre around quite easily. We have designed the shop to cater for all, including children, as we have a small, well-used children's area.

I think I have said before that Transport Models Limited has a great reputation and is now one of the largest and best equipped model shops in the North of England. But for how much longer? And where can we go?

Let me tell you about another customer. Len never married, but his sister tried to control his purchasing of model plant equipment, that is, bulldozers, earth moving machines, hydraulic lifting equipment and other very large vehicles, usually painted yellow. These are generally expensive. Len loved these, but his sister certainly didn't. Such was his fear of drawing his sister's wrath, that whenever he bought new models—and this was often—he would go home, prized possessions in bags, wondering where he could hide them.

Len loved America. He was a lorry driver and once a year would go to America with his brother-in-law and travel in his large American truck, fully equipped with beds, kitchen equipment and home from home utensils. He would later narrate his experiences, which were usually connected to the lorries and vehicles he had seen along the way.

I had not seen Len for some months when he came in to the shop accompanied by his sister, but now with a white stick in his hand. He told me he had been in hospital for a few weeks after losing most of his sight, and was now virtually blind. His sister now had full control of his spending, and only allowed an extra model on his birthday and Christmas. Not long afterwards Len died and, as usual, all his models, including cabinets were brought to me to buy.

His sister brought them to the shop with her adopted daughter. She was absolutely beautiful, honey-coloured skin, about six feet tall, with a high-powered job with an American company. Unfortunately she was divorced, and had a young son about twelve years old. They told me they were going to Spain for a holiday as Len's sister was so upset over his death.

About two months later the sister came to see me with terrible news. On their return from Spain the daughter fell ill and died from a blood clot, probably due to the flight.

That is a sad story and the loss of another truly loyal customer and his beautiful niece. Whenever I see model earthmovers or bulldozers, I think of Len.

Wednesday, September 19 2018
My staff are now putting in their requests for next year's holidays. Will we be here? At least they are optimistic. Still no

news from our landlords, so we have no choice but to keep going.

We are ending the relocation sale next week and are planning our restocking for Christmas. Never say never, so keep going forward. At least our suppliers will be happy and we should be back to our normal patterns of buying and selling. If we have to revert back to selling off the stock again, we can do it.

After reading the earlier part of this book you will have come to the conclusion that I really don't give up. I have neither been clever enough to be a prefect at school, nor chosen to be a captain in the netball team. I have always sat on the outside, willing to join in, but never good enough. I think it is a little late in life to try for a netball team, tennis or even hockey, but I have always said that, when I retire, I will go for drawing lessons. It is apparent to me that retirement is still a time in the future, so I decided I would go on a course now. Apples, pears, landscapes or vases have never appealed to me, but to be able to draw people would be brilliant, so, together will my two daughters, I booked a course at Higham Hall in Cumbria for life drawing. For those who have never heard of this, it is drawing naked people, so we all went last week.

Due to the model suffering from a drastic cold she posed for the first three days fully clothed. It was suggested that if her health deteriorated, I was to be her stand in, but she improved. My elder daughter is quite artistic, so did not have many problems, but my first drawing depicted a lady with a very, very small head, large rotund body, and legs which, if these had been supporting the body, would have collapsed at any time. Now my younger daughter drew as would a five-year-old. The head was large, oval eyes which were touching the hair line, with just one eyeball which was placed in the corner as though looking at me. The nose was large and bulbous. I started laughing, so all in the group came to check the drawing. My daughter's drawings did not improve to any great extent over the length of the course, but the atmosphere in Higham Hall (only our class) was jovial to say the least.

On the last day my younger daughter drew a brilliant hand, so it was decided that, if she wanted to continue with art, she should start with the hand and worked outwards. I have kept the drawing and intend to have it framed. I will put a little note on the back regarding Higham Hall and the highlight of her artistic talents. It should make a very nice Christmas present.

Although the art class was supposed to be one of my 'bucket' items, I know this trial will be viewed, with all my other talents, as very mediocre. But I can draw better now than I did five days prior to going on the course. The three of us have decided, having had such a wonderful bonding three days, to go to another art course in November 2019 called Abstract Art in Landscapes. In other words, an assortment of colours with green and brown at the bottom, with white and blue blobs at the top, which could represent trees, grass, sky and clouds.

There is another course which I think may be beneficial, but would take all my courage to attend. It is called Singing for Tone Deaf People. I never sung a song in my life as I cannot hit the right note to start off with. This could be brilliant.

Just think, when I die, people will say that she tried until the very end. Laser eye surgery, teeth improvements, finally, could draw a picture, and could sing. I am determined to add more items to the bucket list, such as salsa dancing and yoga.

One real pleasure to writing this book is the reaction I have had from readers, One young man, who considers himself to be a dealer, asked to read the book. He buys a lot of items from the shop and I always make sure that there is profit for him when he resells. After reading the book he came into the shop and told me he had been approached by a friend as he knew of some old shop stock in Liverpool. He was going to decline, but asked himself whether 'Elizabeth' would buy. He thought I would at least go to Liverpool to check the items out. It was a disappointing trip, so he thought, as he only bought a box full of prints and frames. Whilst checking the stock he found a drawing which resembled a Lowry. He came to the shop and told me about his find and said that he had taken it to a valuers to see if it was worth anything. If it was, he promised to buy me a large box of chocolates as he only went because he had read the book. The valuers confirmed the sale price as around £700. He then came back and asked me whether or not he should keep the drawing in case it went up in value, or sell. I told him that I would sell, use the money for more stock, and then sell that. Make the money work for you I told him. He kept his word and a large box of chocolates was placed on the counter.

He has been to the shop regularly and keeps me informed regarding his present purchases. I think he will do well.

During my time in business I have always called myself a workaholic. Workaholics do not always make money, but time spent doing the work is very, very expensive. Everything here in Transport Models is in size or number order, so time is not lost in looking for stock. My last story here is regarding my lost millions.

When I was in my early twenties, as I have described before, I could never sunbathe due to my skin colourings. I never tanned, but usually blistered and went bright red. However, a liquid came on to the market which, if applied to the skin, would turn the skin brown. It was colourless, and had a consistency of water. I tried this one day before going out, but ended up with dark patches of gravy coloured skin, with large pale areas where I had failed to apply this colourless solution. I applied household bleach to try and return to my normal colour, but ended with a massive skin rash.

Not to be beaten, I studied this carefully and decided that, if I were to mix this browning liquid with moisturising lotion, then add some Christie's Lanolin Emulsion (to avoid my skin burning) I could apply this liquid evenly. My skin turned a beautiful tan colour, the envy of all my friends at the golf club. In turn I mixed batches and gave them to all and sundry. Was this the first ever tanning lotion that I could have patented? My lost millions.

It is now the 13th of June 2019. I am hoping to have this copy sent to the printers.

Just to give an update on all that has transpired before. There are new tenants now in Oyston Mill, so we are assuming our business will continue at this address for the immediate future. Some of my customers have asked me to put them in my next book. The first is Roland, an absolute gentleman about the same age as me who does not have his own transport, so takes two buses to visit the shop. He has painted stacks of watercolours. I have given him one of mine and he brought me a framed watercolour.

The next customer is Eric. who turns up at the shop with bags and bags of engines, mainly Lima. I pay him and he goes home very happy. The locos are checked by the mechanic, then listed on eBay for sale, and Eric sits at home and buys a lot of these back as he really didn't want to part with them in the first place.

Mr No-name, mentioned in an earlier chapter, carried on buying. He ended up buying a sound locomotive, which is very expensive, around £150. However, he has no track so could not hear the sounds the loco made. Again he brought this back, with other goods, for me to buy back. I have tried to stop him from buying, but he will continue.

I am still working, love the business, my customers and, of course, Mark, my business partner, and the staff who always look after me.

Printed in Poland
by Amazon Fulfillment
Poland Sp. z o.o., Wrocław